Gerard Manley Hopkins

Gerard Manley Hopkins

THE CLASSICAL BACKGROUND
AND CRITICAL RECEPTION
OF HIS WORK

by Todd K. Bender

The Johns Hopkins Press
Baltimore

for
Patricia Ann Bender

Preface

This study deals primarily with the ideas that helped form the intellectual context in which Gerard Manley Hopkins wrote and the context in which, a generation later, his poetry was read. One aim of this investigation is to establish that those two contexts are not interchangeable, for to assume that the basic ideas of the critics are the same as Hopkins' ideas leads to a serious misunderstanding of the poems themselves. This is not proposed as a final analysis of Hopkins' art, but as a first step toward a new critical approach to his poetry.

The classical scholar will perhaps forgive me for presuming to discuss classical poetry in the course of this study if he keeps in mind that in doing so I do not necessarily aim to reconstruct the way a Roman or a Greek scholar would have understood his own literature, but how a Victorian scholar—perhaps at times mistakenly—would tend to understand the style in relation to movements current in English literature. Translations, unless otherwise noted, are my own and are intended only as an explanation of my reading of the original text.

Quotations from Hopkins' unpublished papers are made with the permission of Father Caraman and the Society of Jesus, owner of the copyright. I was able to examine these papers with the assistance of a grant-in-aid from the American Council of Learned Societies. I wish especially to thank

Father Fitzgibbon, the librarian of Campion Hall, and his colleagues for their kind and generous help.

For whatever may be valuable in this book I am indebted to the kind help of many scholars. William Irvine undertook the supervision of my work under the most trying difficulties and gave invaluable encouragement and criticism. Wesley Trimpi read the manuscript during its preparation and offered much incisive criticism, especially concerning rhetorical theories in English and Latin verse. Charles R. Beye's wide knowledge of Latin and Greek literature was very patiently brought to bear on my work, much to my profit. My interest in Hopkins was first aroused by John Crowe Ransom, whose teaching has meant more to me than I can ever acknowledge. Although I have benefited from the help of such scholars, I alone am responsible, of course, for any shortcomings or inaccuracies that may be found in the work.

T. K. B.

Paris
January 1966

Contents

Introduction

The dominant critical evaluation of Hopkins' poetry is based on the assumption that he was a *naïf* poet. Although some studies have been made of the sources of particular elements of his technique, the widespread belief persists that his conception of what poetry ought to be was totally new and detached from previous poetry. We find C. Day Lewis, for example, saying that Hopkins' poetic theories were " a kind of innocent experimenting with words, as a child of genius might invent a new style of architecture while playing with bricks." [1] It is the purpose of this study to show: (1) that the assumption that Hopkins is *naïf* springs, not from an accurate study of his work, but from the nature of the critical position itself, and (2) that Hopkins' apparent innovations in poetic theory could be, at least partially, derivative.

A study of the precedents for Hopkins' practice must take account of the actual state of his learning. His education was classical and theological. In his boyhood, his studies were directed toward the curriculum of classical greats at Oxford in which he took a " first "; his youth was devoted to theological study with the Society of Jesus. His adult profession was twofold—Jesuit priest and professor of Greek literature. Hopkins felt strongly that it was his lifelong duty to study classical literature and theological writing, whereas the study

[1] C. Day Lewis, *A Hope for Poetry* (Oxford: Basil Blackwell, 1934), p. 7.

1

of English poetry was but an indulgence for him. A catalogue of the writers he mentions in his papers shows that he did not neglect his duty nor indulge his inclination excessively. Roberta Holloway, in her unpublished doctoral dissertation, " Some Effects of Classical Study in the Work of Hopkins " (University of California, Berkeley, 1945), tabulates all authors to whom Hopkins actually refers in his papers. Her tabulation indicates that his reading in classical literature and scholarship was extensive and thorough, his knowledge of theological writing and English literature of the nineteenth century wide. But his reading in English before, say, 1750 was limited and to a modern eye unbalanced, and his knowledge of Continental literature of his own time very thin. This pattern is evident in his choice of illustrative examples throughout his prose. The literature he knew most thoroughly was Jesuit and/or Hellenic and/or Victorian.

I. A. Richards, William Empson, and Herbert Read are most responsible for the rapid rise of Hopkins' reputation between the wars. They praise his poetry in terms of its immediacy of utterance, its organic form, and its intuitive nature. These characteristics are manifest, we are told, in the non-logical structure of his poems; his contorted grammar; his obscurity, ambiguity, and toughness of texture; and his imagery, which is sensual, far fetched, and " metaphysical." Hopkins' " The Wreck of the Deutschland " was begun in 1875; I. A. Richards' commendatory essay, " Gerard Hopkins," was published in 1926. It seems, therefore, that Hopkins anticipated by some fifty years what Richards thought poetry ought to be. Herbert Read maintains that he finds Hopkins' work congenial because he did not learn sterile forms from other poets but intuitively invented an organic form of expression. Quite the contrary, it may be that Hopkins' peculiar style could be derived from the writing he knew best.

First we must observe that the criticism written by Richards, Empson, and Read is itself derivative. It is the culmination of an extended movement in art which was motivated by a growing distrust of certain uses of the rational faculty. This distrust, perhaps impelled by the popularization of certain ideas in physical science, caused a shift in the artist's attention from the nominal subject of his work to the operation of the mind which perceives that subject. Hence there was a tendency to shift the criterion for evaluation of art from " How well does a work of art represent the way things really are? " to " How well does a work of art reflect the way the perceiving mind works? " Such a shift in attitude carried with it at least two corollaries. First, the structure of the work must imitate what Read calls the " contour " of ideas crossing the mind; it must be associational. Second, if the artist must give up the advantages of logical structure and syntax, he gains in return what Ford Madox Ford calls the " unearned increment " or what Read calls the " collage effect," the added emotional punch produced by the juxtaposition of logically disparate elements in the work of art. Hopkins foresaw the kind of art his critics were to consider good because he was a pioneer in working out techniques motivated by a set of assumptions about art which subsequent writers were to accept and carry even further. And Hopkins was more precocious in experimenting with the artistic techniques than his contemporaries. Why?

The first mature poem he wrote was by far his most extreme, " The Wreck of the Deutschland," begun in 1875. Stung by his friend Robert Bridges' telling criticism of the poem, he never again went to such lengths in non-logical structure, disjunctive diction, or far-fetched imagery. Unlike Browning, who kept pushing his experiments further and further, Hopkins began with an extreme statement and then retreated from it somewhat. If Hopkins subscribed to the

Victorian ideas that motivated a general tendency toward a new kind of art, why did he, suddenly and at the beginning of his period of poetic creativity, carry this tendency to such an extreme? The reason may lie in the peculiar confluence of Jesuit, classical, and Victorian learning in Hopkins. Here we come to the central question: If Hopkins participated in the Victorian movement toward a new art, is it possible that his study of classical literature encouraged him even further to develop modern techniques? We would perhaps expect the study of *classical* literature to produce a *neoclassical* style that is urbane, limpid, polished, and tightly logical. Is it possible that, instead, the study of Latin and Greek could encourage a style which is quite the opposite—urgent, obscure, unsymmetrical, and non-logical? With regard especially to " The Wreck of the Deutschland," it may be that classical literature could have encouraged his peculiar style in (1) the structure of the poem itself, (2) the structure of sentences within the poem, and (3) the use of sensual and obscure imagery. A study of Hopkins' published and unpublished papers suggests that he found in Pindar a " new " principle of lyric structure, in Latin and Greek hyperbaton a distinctive sentence structure and syntax, and in Martial the explosive word play congenial to Ignatian psychology. Surely we ought to honor the poet the more when we see that he created his revolutionary style, not out of naïveté, but with great deliberation and learning, modifying Latin and Greek practices to build from classical sources a style that was quite different from neoclassical.

I

The Critical Response
to the First and Second
Editions of the Poems

Gerard Manley Hopkins had been dead nearly thirty years
and was virtually unknown in 1918 [1] when Robert Bridges
edited his collected poems. [2] The most extraordinary fact about
Hopkins' early reputation is not that he survived thirty years
of neglect, but that he survived the attention of his friend
Bridges in the preface to the notes of the first edition. [3] After

[1] To my knowledge, there were only seven bits of verse by Hopkins
published in his lifetime: (1) " Winter with the Gulf Stream," published
in *Once a Week*, February 14, 1863; (2) " Silver Jubilee," which Hopkins
tells Bridges in a letter of February 15, 1879, had been published with a
sermon by Fr. John Morris; (3) one stanza of " Morning Midday and
Evening Sacrifice," published in the *Bible Birthday Book*, edited by R. W.
Dixon, 1887; (4) the Latin version of Dryden's " Epigram on Milton " in
Stonyhurst Magazine, July, 1881; (5) three triolets (the first of which is
printed in *Letters* in Note R; the third of which is printed in *Poems*, 68)
in *The Stonyhurst Magazine* IX, March, 1883; (6) Latin version of lines
from Shakespeare in *Irish Monthly* XIV, 1886, p. 628; (7) another Latin
version of lines from Shakespeare in *Irish Monthly* XV, 1887, p. 92.
    After Hopkins' death, " Ad Mariam " appeared in *The Stonyhurst Maga-
zine* LXXII, February, 1894, anonymously. Bridges, of course, introduced
a few of Hopkins' poems into three anthologies: Miles, *Poets and Poetry
of the XIX Century*, 1893; Beeching, *Lyra Sacra* and *A Book of Christmas
Verse*, 1895; and Bridges, *The Spirit of Man*, 1916.
    [2] Gerard Manley Hopkins, *Poems*, edited with notes and a critical preface
by Robert Bridges (London: Oxford University Press, 1918).
    [3] Reprinted in full in W. H. Gardner, *Poems of Gerard Manley Hopkins*,

5

a brief description of the problems of editing, Bridges introduces the reader to Hopkins' work with a discussion of the
poet's "mannerisms." These mannerisms include errors in
"what may be called taste" resulting from "affectation in
metaphor" and from "some perversion of human feeling,"
and errors resulting from "efforts to force emotion into theological or sectarian channels" which are manifest in Hopkins'
"exaggerated Marianism" and the "naked encounter of sensualism and asceticism" to be found in his verse. In addition
to these errors in taste, Bridges proceeds directly to classify
Hopkins' errors in style, which are of such "quality and magnitude as to deny him even a hearing from those who love
continuous literary decorum." Bridges divides the stylistic
errors into the odd and the obscure, maintaining that Hopkins
was deliberately odd but not aware of the obscurity in his
lines. The obscurity stems mainly from the use of ellipsis,
from the use of confusing identical forms of the same word
so that "in aiming at condensation" he carelessly relies on
words that are "grammatically ambiguous," and from the use
of confusing homophones. Then Bridges examines certain
"freakish" and "indefensible" rhymes. There is only one
short paragraph, the second from the end of the essay, which
commends the poems: "Now these are bad faults, and, as I
said, a reader, if he is to get any enjoyment from the author's
genius must be somewhat tolerant of them; and they have a
real relation to the means whereby the very forcible and
original effects of beauty are produced." There follows a
sentence asserting that beauties are to be found in these poems
mixed with crudities, but the third sentence in the paragraph
resumes the attack: "It was an idiosyncracy of this student's
mind to push everything to its logical extreme, and take pleasure in a paradoxical result. . . ." We have, therefore, on the

3rd ed. (London: Oxford University Press, 1948), pp. 202–9. All quotations
of Hopkins' poems are from this edition.

one hand three or four sentences of qualified praise for the poems, accompanied by no supporting examples of good poetry specifically recommended to the reader, and on the other hand three or four pages of carefully organized hostile criticism abundantly illustrated with errors in taste and style isolated from the text for the reader's examination.[4]

[4] The question arises, " Was not the act of editing sufficient endorsement of the poems and evidence of the editor's sympathy? " I think that in the light of the preface we cannot consider Bridges a sympathetic editor. It is possible that his motivation for editing the work was something other than admiration for the poetry. Although Bridges destroyed his letters to Hopkins which were returned to him after Hopkins' death, we can piece together from Hopkins' published letters what the substance of Bridges' correspondence might have been in some cases. It is apparent despite the affectionate language of Hopkins' letters that there were areas of great misunderstanding between the two men. As a result there was certainly a painful lack of sympathy between them at times. For instance, Hopkins sent to Bridges a copy of the first poem he wrote after entering the Society of Jesus, " The Wreck of the Deutschland," and wrote a few notes explaining his technique. Bridges' answer occasioned another long letter from Hopkins filled with further explanation and ending in this way:
" You ask may you call it ' *presumptuous jugglery*. 'No . . .'
" I cannot think of altering anything. Why shd I? I do not write for the public. You are my public and I hope to convert you.
" *You say you would not for any money read my poem again.* Nevertheless I beg you will. Besides money, you know, there is love. If it is obscure do not bother yourself with the meaning but pay attention to the best and most intelligible stanzas. . . . If you had done this you wd. have liked it better and *sent me some serviceable criticisms, but now your criticism is of no use, being only a protest* memoralizing me against my whole policy and proceedings." (Claude Colleer Abbott [ed.], *The Letters of Gerard Manley Hopkins to Robert Bridges*, 2nd rev. impression [London: Oxford University Press, 1955], p. 46. Hereafter cited as *Letters.*)
I have underlined a few phrases which surely must indicate the nature of Bridges' criticism. If he could not bring himself to read the poem twice, it seems strange that he should offer it to the public in a scholarly edition.
But Bridges had an unusually strong feeling of responsibility. He once undertook better than ten years' work in a metrical system of which he did not completely approve in order to fulfill a more or less casual promise. In the Oxford edition of his *Poetical Works* his prefatory note to the poems in classical meter reads,
" These experiments in quantitative verse were made in fulfilment of a promise to William Johnson Stone that I would some day test his theory. His premature death converted my consent into a serious

Bridges' preface dominates the reviews of the first edition of Hopkins' poems. In *The Times Literary Supplement*, January 10, 1919, the reviewer compliments Bridges on his lucid exposition of the poet's faults and promises to speak only of his virtues: "His worst trick is passing from one word to another . . . merely because they are alike in sound. This at its worst produces an effect almost of idiocy, of speech without sense and prolonged merely by echoes. It

obligation. This personal explanation is due myself for two reasons: because I might otherwise appear firstly as an advocate of the system, secondly as responsible for Stone's determination of the length of English syllables." (Robert Bridges, *Poetical Works* [London: Oxford, 1936], p. 408.)

Hopkins, too, died prematurely and his letters often mentioned publication of a poet's works in such a way that Bridges might have felt an obligation to edit Hopkins' poems although he was not an "advocate of the system." Hopkins wrote to Bridges less than two years before Hopkins died:

"By the bye, I say it deliberately and before God, I would have you and Canon Dixon and all true poets remember that fame, the being known, though in itself one of the most dangerous things to man, is nevertheless the true and appointed air, element, and setting of genius and its works. What are works of art for? to educate, to be standards. Education is meant for the many, standards for public use. To produce then is of little use unless what we produce is known, if known widely known, the wider the better, for it is by being known it works, it influences, it does its duty, it does good. We must then try to be known, aim at it, take means to it. And this without puffing in the process or pride in the success. But still. . . . Let your light shine before men that they may see your good works (say, of art) and glorify yr. Father in Heaven (that is, acknowledge that they have an absolute excellence in them and are steps in a scale of infinite and inexhaustible excellence)." (*Letters*, p. 231.)

Although Hopkins wrote this to urge Bridges to publish Bridges' own work more widely, it might have been interpreted by Bridges as a serious obligation to publish Hopkins' work after his death. Father Keating, in 1909, had tried to publish the collected poems of Hopkins, but the manuscripts were in the possession of Bridges and he refused, on the one hand, to give them up and, on the other, to publish them at that time. D. Antony Bischoff in "The Manuscripts of Gerard Manley Hopkins," *Thought*, XXVI (Winter, 1951), pp. 551–80, suggests a reason for Bridges' reticence which, as Bischoff says, has very serious implications. We can only be sure that while Bridges was under some pressure to publish the poems, he did, in fact, edit the texts with a reasonable amount of care and give them to the public. The act of publication therefore does not necessarily represent an endorsement of the work.

seems a bad habit, like stuttering, except that he did not strive against it " (p. 19). But the reviewer concludes that the volume of verse is worth readings despite the " faults wilfully displayed." The review in *The Spectator*, May 10, 1919, is more severe: " The Poet Laureate is responsible for the editing of the poems of the late Gerard Hopkins, and he has done his work with the thoroughness and sympathy that we might expect of him. The poems themselves, despite occasional flashes of illuminating fire, are on the whole disappointing. They are too often needlessly obscure, harsh, and perverse . . . [and] do not seem to us to be worth the pains bestowed on them " (p. 599). It is not only the professional reviewer who accepts Bridges' evaluation. T. S. Omond in *English Metrists* writes, " Readers who enjoy fantastic new would-be developments of metre will study these poems. . . . Others neither intolerant nor unhopeful for new experiments will turn from them with repugnance. The editor's notes are, as always, clear and helpful, expounding his friend's metrical theories, and not infrequently registering dissent from his eccentricity." [5]

The reception of the first edition of the poems was not entirely, however, or even dominantly antagonistic. If these early reviews are all read at a single sitting, one gets an impression not of resentment or hostility, but of bewilderment. The reviewers are quite sure that the poetry *ought* to be bad, but the poetry is not quite what it *ought* to be in many ways. As the reviewer for *The Times Literary Supplement* says, " Mr. Bridges, in his notes, enumerates the defects of Hopkins' poetry," and these defects " are obvious " to any reader. Yet despite the obvious characteristic errors, the reviewers often uneasily acknowledge a strong attraction to the poetry. With regard to " The Wreck of the Deutschland," the reviewer in

[5] T. S. Omond, *English Metrists* (London: Oxford University Press, 1921), p. 263.

The Times Literary Supplement says, " Mr. Bridges calls it a great dragon folded in the gate to forbid all entrance; and indeed, it is difficult. For Hopkins poetry meant difficulty; he wrote it to say more than could be said otherwise; it was for him a packing of words with sense, both emotional and intellectual. The defect of the newest English poetry is that it says too little." He concludes, " You fight your way through the verses yet they draw you on." Edward Sapir's review in *Poetry* is by far the most sympathetic of these early reviews.[6] He finds that " undeniably this poet is difficult. He strives for no innocuous Victorian smoothness." Hopkins' poetry is " most precious " because of its individuality. As for the imagery, " There is hardly a line in these pages that does not glow with some strange new flower divinely picked from his imagination." In short, the early reviews, like Bridges' preface to the poems, combine carefully articulated analyses of errors in taste and style in Hopkins' poetry with simple appreciation and admiration of the poetry itself. The hostile criticism is lucid and precise; the admiration is not explained in any coherent or systematic way.[7]

The book itself sold slowly. There were 750 copies printed in the first edition in 1918. Of these, 50 copies were given away; 180 sold the first year; 240 the second; then about 30 copies a year were sold until 1927, when the demand began to pick up slightly. The initial 750 copies were finally exhausted in 1928, ten years after they came off the press. But a remarkable change in critical opinion greeted the second edition of the poems printed just two years later, in 1930, by the

[6] Edward Sapir, *Poetry*, XVIII (1921), 330–36.
[7] The reviewers themselves often explicitly remark on this quality of their reviews. Thus J. Middleton Murry in " Gerard Manley Hopkins," *Athenaeum*, June, 1919, pp. 425–26, after listing errors in taste throughout the essay concludes, " There is no good reason why we should give characteristic specimens of the poet's obscurity, since our aim is to induce people to read him." Reprinted in *Aspects of Literature* (London: W. Collins & Son, 1920), pp. 52–61.

Oxford University Press and edited by Charles Williams. The reviewer for *The Times Literary Supplement*, December 25, 1930, declares, " Not until his friend the late Poet Laureate, Robert Bridges, edited the first volume of Hopkins' poems in 1918 did the world know that the second half of the nineteenth century had possessed another major poet " (p. 1099). The reviewer then disputes Hopkins' authorship of " Ad Mariam " because it is too feeble to be a product of Hopkins' mature powers. He concludes, ". . . Hopkins is full of strange powers (and an unexhausted technical prowess) which [every modern poet] feels he must assimilate and possess." Unreserved praise for the metrical innovations of which Hopkins is a " great master " and for his " true poetic power of phrase " follow. The review ends with a strong plea for the publication of Hopkins' letters and papers, which, indeed, presently began to be prepared in scholarly editions.

Isidor Schneider reviewing for *The Nation*, April 16, 1930, says:

> The elements of Hopkins' originality are bewildering. He is astonishingly bold with words and with forms of speech; he is free with ellipses, coins new words, breaks them in two, transfers the parts of combined words, as when ' brimful in a flash' becomes ' brim in a flashful'; rhymes internally, alliterates, omits that's and which's to have every word dynamic, and displaces prepositions so that their movement in the sentence adds to their force; combines words to sharpen their rhythm, quicken their meaning, and harmonize their sound. . . . If these innovations strike us at first we must remember that it is the major poetry heightened by them that is his great contribution. Beyond question Hopkins belongs among the great poets of English Literature. The experiments may be taken as evidence of the subtlety and diversity of one of the greatest minds to express itself in poetry in his generation. (p. 458)

The reviews of the second edition of Hopkins' poems stress the freshness and vigor of Hopkins' innovations. In the *Satur-*

day Review of Literature, August 9, 1930, H. L. Binsse writes, " In his day English poetry had reached what seems to many of us an *impasse*. It was not truly manly, truly living. . . . Here at last modern poetry can find the rationale, the convention of freedom it has been seeking " (pp. 33–34). Likewise we read in Hildegard Flanner's review in the *New Republic*, February 4, 1931, " There has been no modern poetry attaining to the amazing effect of lines in Hopkins. . . . He can halt a sentence, a verse, retard it with a broken preposition, then set it spinning with a participle, to gather its own momentum until it collects its own climax . . ." (pp. 331–32). This is, of course, nothing more than praise of the very characteristics of the verse to which Bridges objected. The reviewer continues, " Verbal indulgences, so easily faults of diffuseness, are here less faults than a curious, purposive colliding and jamming an over-lapping and telescoping of images and words in an effort to-ward sustained music and sense."

The reviewers of the second edition maintain an admirably flexible position, in light of the earlier unfavorable reception of the first edition. Lines quoted in 1919 as errors in taste and style are printed once more in 1931 as examples of excellent verse. The pivotal work in this critical movement seems to be I. A. Richards' influential essay, " Gerard Hopkins," pub-lished in *The Dial* in September, 1926. Bridges had found errors of taste and style in the poems; more specifically, he found oddity, obscurity, ambiguity, and paradox. There are two ways to refute this charge. It must be maintained either that the poems do not contain oddity, obscurity, ambiguity, or paradox, or that, although the poems do indeed contain such characteristics, they are not errors at all. Richards chooses to defend oddity, obscurity, ambiguity, and paradox as virtues in poetry:

> Modern verse is perhaps more often too lucid than too
> obscure. It passes through the mind (or the mind passes over
> it) with too little friction and too swiftly for the develop-

ment of the response. Poets who can compel slow reading have thus an initial advantage. The effort, the heightened attention, may brace the reader, and that peculiar intellectual thrill which celebrates the step-by-step conquest of understanding may irradiate and awaken other mental activities more essential to poetry. (p. 195)

Richards sees where his argument is tending, however, and with a tinge of panic at the thought of wholly unlimited iambic confusion he quickly adds, " These are arguments for some slight obscurity in its own right. No one would pretend that the obscurity may not be excessive. It may be distracting, for example. But what is a distraction in a first reading may be non-existent in a second." There is, then, a desirable obscurity and " few poets illustrate this thesis better than Gerard Hopkins who may be described, without opposition, as one of the most obscure of English verse writers." Just as Richards justifies obscurity as a poetic virtue, so he justifies oddity as healthy innovation: " The more the poems are studied, the clearer it becomes that their oddities are always deliberate. They may be aberrations, they are not blemishes. It is easier to see this today since some of his most daring innovations have been, in part, attempted by later poets." After a short explication of " Peace," "(Carrion Comfort)," and " The Windhover " in which Richards finds " an asceticism which fails to reach ecstasy and accepts the failure," he concludes his refutation of the charges of " oddity, of playfulness, of whimsical eccentricity and wantonness " by asserting, " The little that has been written about him has already said too much about this aspect. His work as a pioneer has not been equally insisted upon." [8]

The immediate effect of Richards' essay can be seen, for example, in Henry Morton Robinson's article on Hopkins in

---

[8] The next sentence in the text reads, " It is true that Gerard Hopkins did not fully realize what he was doing to the technique of poetry." We will discuss this statement in some detail presently.

Commonweal, December 28, 1927. Robinson maintains that
the oddity in Hopkins is " pure form " and that " conjecture
yields dark psychical reasons for . . . obscurity " (pp. 869–71).
And, of course, Richards' justification of obscurity as intrinsically valuable underlies most of the reviews of the second
edition of Hopkins' poems wherein Hopkins is praised for the
very characteristics which Bridges criticized. Michael Roberts
in *Poetry*, May, 1932, maintains that the industrial revolution
makes necessary a new kind of poetry, the kind written by
T. S. Eliot and by Hopkins. He grants that we ought to
admire the old poets, but " if, as Mr. Richards suggests, poetry
is to assume some of the functions of religion, it cannot spend
its energy in such futility nor can it deck contemporary life in
romantic trappings. . . . It is necessary at present to emphasize
the need for ' actuality ' in poetry rather than the need for
elegance, for that technical beauty which is independent of
the psychological value of the poet's attitude " (p. 275). It
is clear from subsequent critical writing that Richards' essay
replaced Bridges' critical preface as the dominant evaluation
of Hopkins' work. In a review of an early critical work on
Hopkins in *Commonweal*, April 13, 1934, Harris Downey
says, " Hopkins sought a new mode of expression, and he
perfected that mode; but only time could educate man to
understanding and appreciation. What makes Hopkins a
peculiar poet is what makes him a great poet " (p. 667). He
assumes that the change in attitude toward Hopkins is the
consequence of a better " understanding " of the poet. There
are, of course, other possible reasons for a change in attitude.

Just as Bridges objected to the poetry of Hopkins because
it did not fit his notions of what poetry *ought* to be, so Richards praises the poetry because it seems to fit his preconceived
notion of what poetry *ought* to be. It does not follow necessarily that, because Richards liked the poetry of Hopkins more
than Bridges, Richards understood the poetry any better than

Bridges. Richards' appreciation depends on his peculiar theories of aesthetics developed well before he wrote his essay on Hopkins in 1926. His ideas about art are predicated on a psychological theory of value which, although he continually seems to modify his position, is clearly worked out in *The Principles of Literary Criticism*, 1925. His argument might be paraphrased in this way: A man is born with a set of impulses, or appetites and aversions. These impulses are basically unacceptable to society. That is, on the crudest level, a child has an impulse to eat but he may not steal food from his brother. These initial impulses are repressed and systematized. From birth therefore man's impulses are in conflict: " The conduct of life is throughout an attempt to organize impulses so that success is obtained for the greater number or mass of them, for the most important and weightiest set." [9] Anything is valuable which satisfies an appetite. Although the appetite may be unconscious, the mind can systematize our appetites and find an order of precedence for them. The importance of an impulse is the extent of the disturbance of other impulses in the individual's activities which the thwarting of that impulse involves. That organization of impulses which is least wasteful of opportunities to satisfy human wants is best. Literature is a means for improving our organization of impulses. The artist's work is the ordering of what in most minds is disordered, organizing impulses so as to attain the greatest possible gratification. For this reason alone we find art valuable.

Richards uses this psychological idea of value to reach his theory of aesthetic experience, which might be called his doctrine of mental poise. He assumes that the mind is the nervous system. Every mental event has an origin in the stimulation, a character, and consequences in action or ad-

[9] I. A. Richards, *Principles of Literary Criticism* (London: Routledge Keegan Paul, 1952), p. 46.

justment to action. Stimuli are always preparing the mind for
action without our knowledge. Thus we sit in a garden reading about a centipede biting and jump unexpectedly when a
leaf falls on us. The co-ordination of a number of impulses
is often such that no overt action takes place and the difference
between the intelligent or refined person and the stupid or
crass person is a difference in the extent to which overt action
can be replaced by incipient and imaginal action. Richards
calls these incipient actions " attitudes."

The ordinary man must suppress nine-tenths of his impulses
in order to live. When he feels two conflicting sets of impulses, he must choose to follow whichever appears better.
But the artist can manage two or more sets of impulses at
once. To illustrate his point here, Richards names two groups
of poems. The second group is assumed to be very good
poetry and includes " Ode to a Nightingale," " Proud Maisie,"
" Sir Patrick Spens," " The Definition of Love," and " Noc-
turnall upon S. Lucie's Day." He says of this group of poems:

> The most obvious feature is the extraordinarily [*sic*] hetero-
> geneity of the distinguishable impulses. But they are more
> than heterogeneous, they are opposed. They are such that in
> ordinary, nonpoetic, non-imaginative experience, one or
> other set would be suppressed to give as it might appear freer
> development to the others. . . . Irony in this sense consists
> in bringing in of the opposite, the complementary impulses;
> that is why . . . irony itself is so constantly a characteristic
> of poetry which is [of the highest order].[10]

Richards then digresses to disavow " undue certainty " about
this theory, but continues, " The equilibrium of opposed impulses, which we suspect to be the ground plan of the most
valuable aesthetic responses, brings into play far more of our
personality than is possible in experiences of a more defined
emotion. We cease to be oriented in one definite direction;

[10] *Ibid.,* p. 250.

more facets of the mind are exposed, and, what is the same thing, more aspects of things are able to affect us." [11]

Richards maintains that the mind which can respond to a stimulus through only one narrow channel of interest is severely limited. The true artist will be able to respond simultaneously and coherently through many channels of interest. The true artist is therefore " disinterested " in the sense that he can see things from more than one standpoint and under more than one aspect; he is able to engage more of his personality in the experience. When we meet experience in this way, we see more of events than when we meet experiences in our normal fashion.

> We seem to see " all round " them, to see them as they really are; we see them apart from any particular interest which they may have for us. . . . These characters of aesthetic experiences can thus be shown to be very natural consequences of the diversity of their components. But that so many different impulses should enter in is only what may be expected in an experience whose ground plan is a balance of opposites. For every impulse which does not complete itself in isolation tends to bring in allied systems. The state of irresolution shows this clearly.[12]

But Richards hastens to explain that irresolution is quite different from the state induced by artistic vision: " The difference between any such welter of [irresolute] vacillating impulses and the states of [artistic] composure we are considering may well be a matter of mediating relations between the supporting systems brought in from either side." [13] His interest in balanced systems of thought by which we seem to see all round things is, of course, the theoretical basis for critical interest in ambiguity. Ambiguity in art is the expression of the conflicting sets of impulses which he desires. Richards had expli-

[11] *Ibid.*, p. 251.
[12] *Ibid.*
[13] *Ibid.*

cated " The Windhover " in his 1926 essay and thereby established it as a focus of attention in the study of Hopkins. In
Practical Criticism he uses Hopkins' " Spring and Fall " as the
subject for a set of protocols and is mildly outraged that only
31 per cent of his subjects praised the poem. Although, since
Richards omitted the accent mark on the final syllable of the
first word in the poem, we must wonder whether he had
any idea how many syllables Hopkins intended the word
" Margaret " to have, and hence any idea of the poem's meter.

The direct influence of Richards on Empson can be seen
when Empson picks up Richards' examples, " The Windhover " and " Spring and Fall," in *Seven Types of Ambiguity*.
He gives " Spring and Fall " as an example of ambiguity
arising from accent: " You may be intended, while reading
a line one way, to be conscious that it could be read another;
so that if it is to be read aloud it must be read twice; or you
may be intended to read it in some way different from the
colloquial speech-movements so as to imply both ways at
once." [14] He then demonstrates that it is difficult to assign one
definite meaning to the poem. Empson sees " The Windhover " as an example of the use of poetry to convey indecision. About the lines

> Brute beauty and valour and act, oh, air, pride, plume here
>   Buckle! AND the fire that breaks from thee then, a billion
> Times told lovelier, more dangerous, O my chevalier!

he says,

> We seem to have a clear case of the Freudian use of opposites,
> where two things thought of as incompatible, are desired
> intensely by different systems of judgment, are spoken of
> simultaneously by words applying to both; both desires are
> thus given a transient and exhausting satisfaction, and the
> two systems of judgment are forced into open conflict
> before the reader. Such a process, one might imagine, could

[14] William Empson, *Seven Types of Ambiguity* (New York: Meridian,
1955), p. 167.

pierce to regions that underlie the whole structure of our thought; could tap the energies of the very depths of the mind.[15]

This is a clear statement of Richards' theory of mental poise and demonstrates the practical application of the theory. To praise Hopkins because the ambiguities of his verse create a state of mental poise is, of course, to divert critical interest from what went on in the author's mind when he wrote the poem to what goes on in the critic's mind when he reads the poem. Richards' praise of Hopkins implies a subjective approach to his poetry and indeed such an approach has been dominant ever since the second edition of the poems was printed. Even critics who maintain that they disagree with Richards and Empson tend to approach the poetry in terms of exploring what goes on in the reader's mind rather than in terms of reconstructing Hopkins' meaning. Thus a critic ostensibly so hostile toward Empson's work as to say, " One cannot doubt that Mr. Empson's treatment of Hopkins was a conscious, strained, and stupid effort to make his criticism, if it may be so called, strengthen the title of his book," [16] will nevertheless accept the critical assumptions behind Empson's work so as to find it a helpful bit of information that the word " dauphin " sounds like the word " dolphin " and that this contradictory meaning enriches our reading of " The Windhover." And taking a hint from that critic, R. W. Ayers completes the exegesis.[17] He reads the lines,

> I caught this morning morning's minion, king-
> dom of daylight's
> dauphin, dapple-dawn-drawn Falcon, in
> his riding
> Of the rolling level underneath him steady air, and striding

[15] *Ibid.*, p. 255.
[16] Harris Downey, " A Poem Not Understood," *Virginia Quarterly*, II (1935), 509.
[17] R. W. Ayers, " Hopkins' ' The Windhover,' a Further Simplification," *Modern Language Notes*, LXXI (Dec., 1956), 577–84.

> High there, how he rung upon the rein of a wimpling wing
> In his ecstasy! then off, off forth on swing,
> As a skate's heel sweeps smooth on a bow-bend . . .

and notices the following secondary meanings: "Skate" means a kind of fish or ray, *raja batis*. "Heel" means the inclination of the fish from horizontal in the water, as a boat heels. "Bow-bend" means the curve of the bow of a ship or a motion which describes such a curve. "Rolling level" means the surface of the sea. And so on. All of this is excused by saying that whether the author intended such a meaning or not, the poem will seem better if we realize that such meanings are possible. The belief that ambiguity is intrinsically valuable leads to the derision of resolution of Hopkins' ambiguity, that is a resolution of his apparent "value," through historical research. The criticism of Hopkins which is most common is often strangely negligent of the author. For example, of the lines

> And though the last lights off the black West went
> Oh, morning, at the brown brink eastward, springs.

W. A. M. Peters writes, "I take 'springs' not only to be synonymous with, though much more expressive than, 'rises'; it calls up the likeness of the morning to spring-time. *Intentional or not, this suggestion certainly enhances the beauty and freshness that these lines breathe.*" [18] Since Richards desires a poetry which will cause a psychical poise and since this psychical poise occurs in the mind of the reader, there is a tendency implicit in Richards' criticism to study the effect of the poetry on the mind of the reader rather than to study the mind of the author. If a critic finds ambiguity desirable, he tends to hunt for alternative meanings for a line rather than to try to resolve the ambiguities by historical criticism, and

[18] W. A. M. Peters, *Gerard Manley Hopkins* (London: Oxford, 1948), p. 158. My italics.

it is certainly true that the study of Hopkins has tended to extend rather than limit the possible meanings of a poem like " The Windhover," for example.

As one important consequence of Richards' criticism, then, was to emphasize study of the effect of the poetry on the reader's mind at the expense of study of the poet's mind, so another consequence was to emphasize the study of the innovations in Hopkins' verse at the expense of the study of the derivative elements in his work. There is a strong tendency to treat these innovations as intuitive, necessarily detached from all literary tradition, and certainly not acquired by the poet from study of previous writers. Hopkins, who was once called the " Star of Balliol " because of his brilliance as a student of classical literature, is thereby represented in the bizarre guise of a Roman Catholic Corydon tending his parish flock and in his intellectual isolation warbling rude but powerful woodnotes wild. In this fashion Cecil Day Lewis in *A Hope For Poetry* in 1934 classifies Hopkins as " predominantly what I have called a ' *naïf* ' poet." [19] He finds that Hopkins " is difficult to connect with anything in the past," and that he is " without affinities." For " poets may be divided into two classes; those who assimilate a number of influences and construct an original speech from them, and those whose voice seems to come out of the blue, reminding us of nothing we have heard before." [20] Hopkins, we are told, belongs to the class of poets whose voice reminds us of no previous poet. Day Lewis finds Hopkins so totally new that he " should even go so far as to call Hopkins an unconscious revolutionary." [21] Although he praises Hopkins very highly, the characteristics for which he does so can be the object of scorn. G. M. Young, for instance, says of the identical characteristics, " The root of his [Hopkins'] error lay in an ignorance of the subject so profound that he was not aware that there was anything to

[19] P. 8.
[20] *Ibid.*, p. 7.
[21] *Ibid.*, p. 8.

know." [22] But it is important to note that whether they praise or damn Hopkins, both writers assume that Hopkins was innocent of any significant knowledge of literary traditions. Although Day Lewis praises the alleged freedom, whereas Young deplores the ignorance of decorum, both agree that Hopkins was detached from any literary tradition. Because Day Lewis is more sympathetic to the poetry, it does not necessarily follow that he understands it better than Young. It is possible that both critics make a faulty assumption when they assert that Hopkins was naïve in literary matters.

Day Lewis considers the immediate ancestors of the poetry written after World War I to be Hopkins, Owen, and Eliot. These poets have in common, he asserts, an admirable freedom from sterile tradition; they have rediscovered the source of true poetry. The most vigorous proponent of this argument is perhaps Herbert Read and he is strongly influenced by T. E. Hulme's *Speculations*, which he edited in 1924. Hulme himself admired Henri Bergson and says, " If one wanted to give the broadest possible description of the aim that Bergson pursues in all his work one would have to say that it was an endeavor to prove that we arrive at a certain picture of the nature of reality, not because such is, as a matter of fact, the nature of things, but because a certain inveterate tendency of the mind distorts things in that direction." [23] Hulme interprets Bergson to mean that the " ordinary use of the logical intellect " distorts rather than reveals because the " logical intellect " is so constructed that it must view the world as " being in reality a vast machine." Hulme concludes, " To obtain a complete picture of reality it is necessary to employ another faculty of the mind, which . . . Bergson calls intuition. It is useless then to dream of one science of nature, for there

[22] G. M. Young, "Forty Years of Verse," *London Mercury*, XXXV (1936), 120.

[23] T. E. Hulme, *Speculations* (New York: Harcourt, Brace & Co., 1924), p. 173.

must be two—one dealing with matter which will be built up by the intellect, and the other dealing with certain aspects of life which will employ intuition." [24]

Hulme therefore maintains that there are two methods of thinking: the one rational or mechanical, the other vital and more instinctive. He then makes his well-known distinction between extensive and intensive manifolds. The rational or mechanical method of thinking can deal only with extensive manifolds; it explains or analyzes. " It persists in unfolding things out in space. It is not satisfied unless it can see every part." [25] Hulme says we know " that the intellect which always thinks, as it were, in space, which always insists in having a clear diagram or picture, insists in analyzing complex things into an aggregate of separate elements which we call extensive manifolds. In order that the intellect may be able to completely grasp reality, it is necessary that reality should be composed entirely in this way." [26] But, Hulme continues, is it not possible that there is some " interpenetration of parts which cannot be separated," [27] or analyzed, which he calls an intensive manifold. He poses two questions: "(1) Is there such a faculty as intuition, as distinct from the intellect, which enables one to know certain things without being able to analyze or to state them? (2) Are there as a matter of fact existing in nature any such things as intensive manifolds? " [28] Hulme finds that the mind itself offers an example of an intensive manifold. We can name an emotion, for instance, calling it *hate* or *love*, but we cannot analyze its elements: " To describe accurately, then, any emotion—to give it accurately and not approximately—you would have to describe at the same time the whole personality in which it occurs, which is only another way of saying that mental life forms a whole

[24] *Ibid.*, p. 174.
[25] *Ibid.*, p. 178.
[26] *Ibid.*, p. 180.
[27] *Ibid.*
[28] *Ibid.*, p. 182.

which cannot be analyzed into parts." [29] But although we cannot analyze hate or love we are aware of the flow of mental life; we know that hate and love exist. We cannot define or separate all the multiple elements conditioning our attitudes, but we intuitively know that these attitudes exist. Therefore, Hulme concludes, we know that intensive manifolds exist which defy logical analysis and we know that it is possible to be aware of these intensive manifolds by intuitive means.

Hulme's analysis forms the basis for Herbert Read's criticism of Hopkins, which, in turn, is largely responsible for the subsequent emphasis on Hopkins' detachment from literary traditions. Read sees the history of modern poetry as a record of revolt against sterile forms. Wordsworth began the revolt, but " against the magnitude of Wordsworth's experiment all the minor tinkerings of the nineteenth century are as nothing—until we come to Browning and Gerard Manley Hopkins. . . . It was with the school which Hulme started and Pound established that the revolution begun in Wordsworth was finally completed." [30] In explaining this revolution, Read distinguishes between organic form and abstract form:

> *Organic Form:* When a work of art has its own inherent laws, originating with its very invention and fusing in one vital unity both structure and content, then the resulting form may be described as *organic*.
> *Abstract form:* When an organic form is stabilized and repeated as a pattern, and the intention of the artist is no longer related to the inherent dynamism of an inventive act, but seeks to adapt content to predetermined structure, then the resulting form may be described as *abstract*.[31]

It is, he maintains, the organic form which is vital in poetry. Read then distinguishes between *character* and *personality*,

[29] *Ibid.*, p. 185.
[30] Herbert Read, *Collected Essays in Literary Criticism* (London: Faber & Faber Ltd., 1938), p. 48.
[31] *Ibid.*, p. 19.

relying on Freud's division of the human mind into conscious, pre-conscious, and unconscious-repressed states. A *character*, as for example in Theophrastus, is a consistent type. *Character* therefore results from the power to keep a selected motive dominant throughout life. It implies inhibition, the suppression of certain desires and memories of experience not consistent with the characteristic motivation. *Personality*, on the other hand, is the full complex of conscious, pre-conscious, and unconscious-repressed elements in the mind. *Personality* and *character* therefore are by nature conflicting forces and art can be produced only when the personality escapes from the inhibitions of character.

> Character, in short, is an impersonal ideal which the individual selects and to which he sacrifices all other claims, especially those of the sentiments or emotions. It follows that character must be placed in opposition to personality, . . . That is, indeed, the opposition I wish to emphasize; and when I have said further that all poetry, in which I include all lyrical impulses whatsoever, is the product of personality, and therefore inhibited in a character, I have stated the main theme. . . .[32]

The intermittency of creative activity in an artist thus proves that creative activity can occur only when the *personality* overcomes the *character*, when the artist sees beyond his conscious state of mind. Read continues, " Such lights come, of course, from the latent memory of verbal images in what Freud calls the pre-conscious state of mind; or from the still obscurer state of the unconscious, in which are hidden, not only the neural traces of repressed sensations, but also those inherited patterns which determine our instincts." [33]

Read maintains that such an intuition cannot be expressed except in a form dictated by the laws of its own origination.

---

[32] *Ibid.*, pp. 29–30.   [33] *Ibid.*, p. 38.

" It thus comes about that every poet . . . —from Wordsworth to Hopkins or Mr. Eliot—has to wear the trappings of a rebel, and what is the assertion of a law of discipline is treated as a declaration of independence." [34] The form of all true art must therefore be intuitive, not acquired or learned through study or even be premeditated. Such an argument is necessarily a defense of primitive art and Read does not hesitate to quote Vico with admiration and to conclude, " Man, before he has arrived at the stage of forming universals, forms imaginary ideas. Before he reflects with a clear mind, he apprehends with faculties confused and disturbed; before he can articulate, he sings; before speaking in prose, he speaks in verse: before using technical terms, he uses metaphors, and the metaphorical use of words is as natural to him as that which we call natural." [35] Read directs his readers into the subconscious in search of the essence of poetry, and all that is to be found there is Macaulay lecturing on Milton. We could take sentences from Macaulay's essay on Milton published in the *Edinburgh Review* in 1825 and insert them almost at random into Read's text without impairing the flow of the argument. For example, Macaulay asserts "that most orthodox article of literary faith, . . . the earliest poets are generally the best. . . ."

> But language, the machine of the poet, is best fitted to his purpose in its rudest state. Nations, like individuals, first perceive, then abstract. They advance from particular images to general terms. Hence the vocabulary of an enlightened society is philosophical, that of a half-civilized people is poetical. . . . In proportion as men know more and think more, they look less at individuals and more at classes. They therefore make better theories and worse poems.

Now, such a defense of primitive art implies a defense of obscurity. For if our modern language is abstracted so as to

[34] *Ibid.*, p. 41.   [35] *Ibid.*, p. 98.

distort " reality," then modern language as it is normally used
will be inadequate to express the poet's intuition. Read says,
" It is a mistake, therefore, to ask a poet to explain his poems.
. . . The poet has created in words an objective equivalence
of his emotional experience: the words may not make sense,
but they make emotion—follow the contour of the thought." [36]
Or again, " We see . . . that essentially obscurity lies not in
the poet but in ourselves. We are clear and logical at the cost
of being superficial or inexact. The poet, more exactingly,
seeks absolute precision of language and thought, and the
exigencies of this precision demand that he should exceed the
limits of customary expression, and therefore *invent*—invent
sometimes words, more frequently new uses of words, most
frequently phrases and figures of speech which reanimate
words." [37] Read finds that obscurity in poetry signifies hon-
esty on the part of the poet; because his words seem to make
no sense, we know that he is groping beyond the super-
ficialities of ordinary speech. For this reason Hopkins is
" amongst the most vital poets of our time, and his influence
will reach far into the future of English poetry." [38]

Read does not neglect to quote Plato in the *Ion* on the
inspired or possessed nature of the poet.[39] And this line of
thought has a great influence on general criticism of Hopkins.
We find an early, and extreme, example of approval for an
alleged " insane excitement " in Hopkins' verse in *Poetry*,
1929, wherein the critic admires the " rush of magically associated words and phrases, arranged by instinct and not by
reason, and so inevitably welded together." [40]

The reversal of opinion about Hopkins' verse which occurred between the issue of the first edition of Hopkins' poems
in 1918 and the second edition in 1930 carries with it certain

---

[36] *Ibid.*, p. 100. [38] *Ibid.*, p. 353.
[37] *Ibid.*, p. 98. [39] *Ibid.*, p. 133.
[40] Jessica North, " Quality in Madness," *Poetry*, XXXIV (Aug., 1929),
271.

assumptions about and attitudes toward Hopkins and his work. First, the assumption that the poems produce a state of psychical poise induces critics to turn from study of the mind of the poet to a study of the mind of the reader. Second, the assumption that Hopkins' oddity is innovation aimed at correcting the inadequacy of the common Victorian poetic idiom leads to the assumption that Hopkins was *naïf*, primitive, detached from all significant literary traditions. To deny these two assumptions was to deny the value of Hopkins' verse.

The pervading influence of these ideas is apparent in Elsie Elizabeth Phare's *The Poetry of Gerard Manley Hopkins: A Survey and Commentary*,[41] which, if we except G. F. Lahey's sketchy biographical account [42] published slightly before the second edition of the poems, is the first full-length critical study of Hopkins. Read, Richards, and Empson were the most forceful proponents of Hopkins because of his allegedly meaningful ambiguity and primitive artistry. Phare's book was, in fact, written as a doctoral dissertation under Richards and it is perhaps not surprising that the book is mainly an extension and application of Richards' ideas. The assumptions of Read, Richards, and Empson are accepted along with their evaluation of the poet. Phare begins her work with the assumption that Hopkins is for the most part detached from identifiable literary traditions. She observes that the French are an orderly nation and delight in the discovery that Lautréamont fits between Rimbaud and Baudelaire in the scheme of their literary tradition. But Hopkins is in general detached from such a scheme; " with Hopkins this [literary classification] is extraordinarily difficult. No bookseller's window, so far as I know, has ever been placarded

[41] Elsie Elizabeth Phare (Mrs. Austin Duncan-Jones), *The Poetry of Gerard Manley Hopkins: A Survey and Commentary* (Cambridge: Cambridge University Press, 1933).

[42] G. F. Lahey, S. J., *Gerard Manley Hopkins* (London: Oxford University Press, 1930).

with the discovery that the place of Hopkins is between so-and-so and such-and-such, and we may doubt whether it is likely to be." [43] Thus we begin with Read's assumption that insofar as Hopkins was an artist, he was detached from tradition. Phare uses Read's theory, that intermittency of production in an artist is due to the suppression of personality by character, to explain the periods of poetic silence in Hopkins' career: "Herbert Read suggests in his *Form in Modern Poetry* that fancy may be identified with phantasy proceeding from the unconscious as a balance or compensation for instincts repressed in the interests of character. This is a suggestion which would fit in with Hopkins' circumstances." [44] Phare reasons that while Hopkins was undergoing the "arduous process of becoming a Jesuit," he was subjecting his personality to his character and therefore could not be artistically productive. She also uses Richards' theory of psychic poise to justify obscurity in Hopkins' poetry: "As Mr. Richards has said, Hopkins deliberately makes it impossible for the reader to hurry over his lines, and he demands to be read slowly, and with ear, so that the full content of his poetry may have time to appear. The unusual richness and complexity of his verse makes this demand not only justifiable, but necessary." [45] Phare maintains that Richards must be correct because the great poets have all failed in their intention if they intended to be unambiguous in their logical meaning. She asserts, "Tennyson, a sufficiently lucid poet, when asked whether he meant this or that by a certain phrase in one of his poems admitted that he meant both, and Mr. Empson in his *Seven Types of Ambiguity* has argued that ambiguity is the backbone of most good poems." [46] Thus Phare assumes that good poetry produces a state of mental poise and that

---

[43] Phare, *Poetry*, p. 1.
[44] *Ibid.*, p. 18.

[45] *Ibid.*, p. 94.
[46] *Ibid.*, p. 95.

ambiguity is the expression of that poise. Her treatment of
" The Windhover," for example, clearly shows that she begins
from Richards' premises: " *The Windhover*, like most very
great poetry, has had many different meanings attributed to it.
This is partly because it is so rich in significance and partly
because the poet's state of mind is one in which two contradictory moods are held in equipoise and the reader can make
one or the other predominate as he chooses." [47]   Phare then
explains her reading of the poem for several pages, but concludes that it would be improper to limit the meaning to her
interpretation. "But on comparing my reading with Dr.
Richards' much fuller and more fluid interpretation of the
poem it becomes evident that the former, in spite of all my
efforts to the contrary, remains purely personal." [48]   She therefore quotes Richards' version for several pages. Then, finding
that version insufficiently flexible, she quotes Empson on
" The Windhover " for about two more pages, but concludes,
" The associations suggested by Mr. Empson to me limit
unnecessarily the implications of the sonnet." [49]   Phare's book,
the first important full-length study of Hopkins, reveals that
the author adopts not only the evaluation of Hopkins' poetry
which was proposed by Read, Richards, and Empson, but also
the assumptions and critical methods implied in that particular
evaluation. The emphasis is given to the way the poetry
affects a peculiar reader's mind and to the detachment of
Hopkins from traditional literary forms.

Paradoxically enough, while critics were praising Hopkins
for his freedom from sterile tradition, for the organic nature
of his forms, poets were eagerly assimilating and copying
Hopkins' forms in their own poems. We can open Auden's
Collected Shorter Poems almost at random and hear Hopkins'
influence. Thus Auden says,

---

[47] *Ibid.*, p. 131.   [49] *Ibid.*, p. 138.
[48] *Ibid.*, p. 133.

> Happy the hare at morning, for she cannot read
> The Hunter's waking thoughts, lucky the leaf
> Unable to predict the fall, lucky indeed.[50]

echoing lines like Hopkins'

> I wake and feel the fell of dark, not day.
> What hours, O what black hours we have spent
> This night! what sights you, heart, saw; ways you went!

Thus the opening of Day Lewis' *Magnetic Mountain*,

> Now to be with you, elate, unshared,
> My kestral joy, O hovered in wind,
> Over the quarry furiously at rest
> Chaired on shoulders of shouting wind.
> Where's that unique one, wind and wing married,
> Aloft in contact of earth and ether;
> Feathery my comet, Oh too often
> From heav'n harried by carrion cares

shows a curious mixtures of " The Windhover " and diction
from other lines from Hopkins. Thus the concluding lines
from Hopkins' " Felix Randal,"

> When thou at the random grim forge, powerful amidst peers,
> Didst fettle for the great grey drayhorse his bright and batter-
> ing sandal!

might well serve as the opening lines for T. H. White's *A
Dray Horse,*

> Meek Hercules, passion of arched power bowed to titanic
> affection;
> Docile though vanquishing, stout-limber in vastness, plunging
> and spurning thy road;
> Taughten thy traces, triumph past me, take thy shattering
> direction
> Through misty Glasgow, dragging in a tremendous beer-wagon
> thy cobble-thundering load.

[50] W. H. Auden, " Culture," *Collected Shorter Poems* (London: Faber &
Faber, 1950), p. 62.

But we must note that it is the technique of Hopkins which is emulated, not his ideology. We can easily name a half dozen modern poets whose work reflects the rhythm, or repetition of sound, or diction of Hopkins, but how many poets can we name who were influenced by Hopkins to join the Jesuits— or even to read classical greats? Matthiessen has noted that modern poets often have used Hopkins' techniques to express Whitman's ideas.[51] The central topic of much of Hopkins' most eccentric poetry is personal. His followers often copy these eccentricities in writing about social problems. The critics praise Hopkins' form as organic while the poets copy it as abstract form.

[51] F. O. Matthiessen, *American Renaissance* (New York: Oxford University Press, 1941), pp. 584–92.

II

The Publication of the Prose and a Note on the Unpublished Notebooks

The rising interest in Hopkins following the second edition of his poems and its favorable critical reception led to the collection and publication of his scattered personal papers. Claude Colleer Abbott edited *The Letters of Gerard Manley Hopkins to Robert Bridges* and *The Correspondence of Gerard Manley Hopkins and Richard Watson Dixon*[1] in 1935; Humphrey House edited *The Notebooks and Papers of Gerard Manley Hopkins*[2] in 1937; and Abbott continued his work with the *Further Letters of Gerard Manley Hopkins*.[3] As more papers were discovered, it was presently necessary to re-work this material with additions into *The Journals and Papers of Gerard Manley Hopkins*[4] edited by Humphrey House and completed by Graham Storey in 1959 and *The*

[1] Claude Colleer Abbott (ed.), *The Correspondence of Gerard Manley Hopkins and Richard Watson Dixon* (London: Oxford University Press, 1935). Hereafter cited as *Correspondence.*

[2] Humphrey House (ed.), *The Notebooks and Papers of Gerard Manley Hopkins* (London: Oxford University Press, 1937). Hereafter cited as *Notebooks and Papers.*

[3] Claude Colleer Abbott, *Further Letters of Gerard Manley Hopkins* (London: Oxford University Press, 1938). Hereafter cited as *Further Letters.*

[4] Humphrey House (ed.), *The Journals and Papers of Gerard Manley Hopkins* (London: Oxford University Press, 1959). Hereafter cited as *Journals and Papers.*

Sermons and Devotional Writings of Gerard Manley Hopkins [5] edited by Christopher Devlin in the same year. It is much to the credit of the editor, and indeed the author, of these papers that the two attempts at a biography of Hopkins by Lahey [6] and Ruggles [7] seem remarkably inadequate when compared to the raw material in the volumes of correspondence and papers. *Le poète Gérard Manley Hopkins* by Jean-George Ritz was published too recently for detailed treatment here. Its appearance does not alter the general state of our biographical knowledge of Hopkins. Indeed, Ritz's study emphasizes once more the almost insurmountable difficulty of this subject. Louise Bogan, reviewing one of the early volumes, expresses the typical response to the published prose when she says with some awe, " The man was all of a piece." [8] The publication of Hopkins' prose served to confirm his rising fame and at the same time posed new problems of interpretation.

As Hopkins' reputation spread, certain central questions about him became defined so that the most spirited debate revolved around a few main topics. These topics, of course, are not all equally profitable to debate—some have little relation to Hopkins' poetry, and others have little to do with him at all in that they are simply an excuse for an attack on or a defense of Christianity or the Jesuit discipline and thus are of limited literary interest. Most of the studies can be classified in one of five categories: (1) biographical studies of the relation of the two vocations, priest and poet, in Hopkins; (2) studies of ideological influences on Hopkins; (3)

[5] Christopher Devlin (ed.), *The Sermons and Devotional Writings of Gerard Manley Hopkins* (London: Oxford University Press, 1959). Hereafter cited as *Sermons and Devotional Writings*.

[6] Lahey, *Gerard Manley Hopkins*.

[7] Eleanor Ruggles, *Gerard Manley Hopkins, A Life* (New York: W. W. Norton, 1944).

[8] Louise Bogan, "*Further Letters of Gerard Manley Hopkins*; a Review," *The Nation*, CXLVII (July 30, 1938), 111.

studies of stylistic influences on Hopkins' verse; (4) defini-
tions of Hopkins' peculiar terminology and ideas; and (5)
exegesis of particular poems.

Hopkins himself felt that there was a conflict between the
vocation of a priest and that of a poet. He wrote to Dixon
on October 5, 1878, " You ask, do I write verse myself. What
I had written I burnt before I became a Jesuit and resolved
to write no more, as not belonging to my profession, unless
it were by the wish of my superiors; so for seven years I
wrote nothing but two or three little presentation pieces which
occasion called for." [9] Just as there can be no doubt that
Hopkins felt that the two vocations conflicted, there can be
no doubt which vocation he valued more. When Dixon heard
that Hopkins was about to enter his tertianship or second
noviceship, Dixon expressed some concern over Hopkins'
great sacrifices. Hopkins promptly replied,

> My mind is here more at peace than it has ever been and I
> would gladly live all my life, if it were so to be, in as great
> or a greater seclusion from the world and be busied only
> with God. But in the midst of outward occupations not only
> the mind is drawn away from God, which may be at the call
> of duty and be God's will, but unhappily the will too is
> entangled, worldly interests freshen, and worldly ambitions
> revive. The man who in the world is as dead to the world as
> if he were buried in the cloister is already a saint. But this
> is our ideal.[10]

Hopkins believed that his vocation as a poet must be kept
subordinate to his work as a priest, to what he believed to be
the salvation of his soul. This conviction, that the poet must
be subordinate to the priest, prompted Hopkins to avoid
publication of his verse. The danger of publication, except
at the suggestion of a superior, he felt, was that it might divert
the mind from God's work to a search for worldly success.

[9] *Correspondence*, p. 14.
[10] *Ibid.*, p. 75.

Although we can perhaps see the temptation of publication struggling with Hopkins' will, in almost every case Hopkins forcefully rejects the possibility unless he feels that publication is in the service of his order, that is to say in the service of God. Thus he replies to Dixon's proposal to send some of his verses to a local paper, "Pray do not send the piece to the paper: I cannot consent to, I forbid its publication. You must see that to publish my manuscript against my expressed wish is a breach of trust. Ask any friend and he will tell you the same." [11] A great deal of effort has been expended discussing the conflict of vocations in Hopkins, although Hopkins' papers deal with the matter directly. The debate over the effect of the conflict can be divided into two categories: argument about the effect of the conflict on Hopkins the man and about the effect of the conflict on Hopkins' poetry. The debate about the effect on Hopkins, the man, of the conflict between priest and poet seems to be of no real interest to the literary scholar. On this topic we find Jesuits arguing with poets over whether it is better for a man to be a Jesuit or to be a poet. It seems obvious from Hopkins' papers that he refrained from writing poetry at times because he was a priest. Some scholars have lamented this lost bulk of unwritten poems. It has been said that "the choice of the Jesuits was made at the cost of a severe and heavy sacrifice; the sacrifice of his own poetic talent." [12] To this charge a Jesuit writer replies, "Let it be plainly stated then at the outset: religious orders have no crying need of poets; nor, yet again, craving for the honor of their company. Be the poets of major, minor, or mediocre attainments, religious orders flourish grandly like the cedars of Lebanon without them. With them they continue to do so provided the poets

[11] *Ibid.*, p. 30.
[12] John Gould Fletcher, "Gerard Manley Hopkins—Priest or Poet?" *American Review*, VI (1936), 331–46.

in question rest content with their chosen common lot." [13] It is apparent that the argument conducted in these terms is not really about Hopkins at all but about the proper conduct of a man's life. When we turn from a consideration of the conflict's effect on the man to a consideration of its effect on the verses of Hopkins, the argument seems to evaporate. John Pick's *Gerard Manley Hopkins: Priest and Poet* [14] is the first full-length study maintaining that priest and poet are inseparable in him. The question then arises whether his verse is valuable because of the priestly vocation of the poet or in spite of that vocation. On the one hand, Austin Warren says, " My own conclusion is that Hopkins' constant tension, the desire to be an artist and the desire to be a saint, was necessary to his achievement as a poet. Had he written with the facility and fecundity of most Victorians (his friends included) he might have been as undistinguished. He had early ease; he needed to learn to write under difficulty,—to theorize, ponder, wait more often than compose." [15] On the other hand, F. R. Leavis asserts, " It seems reasonable to suppose that if he had had the encouragement he lacked he would have devoted to poetry a good deal of the energy that (for the last years of his life a painfully conscientious Professor of Greek) he distributed, in a strenuous dissipation that undoubtedly had something to do with his sense of being time's eunuch and never producing, between the study of music, musical composition, drawing, and such task-work as writing a ' popular account of Light and Ether.' For he was certainly a born writer." [16]

[13] Chester A Burns, S. J., " Gerard Manley Hopkins, Poet of Ascetic and Aesthetic Conflict," *Immortal Diamond*, ed. Norman Weyand (New York: Sheed and Ward, 1949), p. 176.

[14] John Pick, *Gerard Manley Hopkins: Priest & Poet* (London: Oxford University Press, 1942).

[15] Austin Warren, " Gerard Manley Hopkins," *Gerard Manley Hopkins*, by the Kenyon Critics (Norfolk: New Directions Books, 1945), p. 14.

[16] F. R. Leavis, " Metaphysical Isolation," *Gerard Manley Hopkins*, by the Kenyon Critics, p. 132.

The issue at debate seems to be whether or not Hopkins would
have written a more valuable body of work if he had lived a
radically different life, if, in fact, he had been a different
man. The number of scholars who have written on one side
or the other of this debate testifies to the issue's popularity,
which doubtless is due in part to its delightful unverifiability.

When we turn from the priest-poet debate to studies of the
sources of his ideas, the ideological studies seem disproportionately sparse. Christopher Devlin was the first writer to
point out a possible relationship between Hopkins and Duns
Scotus.[17] Since Scotus is one of the most neglected of England's
great philosophers, any study of him is welcome, but surely
scholars subsequent to Devlin have overemphasized the influence of Scotus on Hopkins. First, as all responsible scholars
admit, the ideas of Hopkins are fortuitously congruent to
those of Scotus rather than derived from him. The earliest
mention of Scotus occurs in Hopkins' entry for July 19,
1872: "After the examinations we went for our holiday out
to Douglas in the Isle of Man Aug. 3. At this time I had first
begun to get hold of the copy of Scotus on the Sentences in
the Baddely library and was flush with a new stroke of en-
thusiasm. It may come to nothing or it may be a mercy from
God. But just then when I took in any inscape of the sky
or sea I thought of Scotus." [18] Now, Scotus is most commonly
used to explain Hopkins' terms such as *instress* or *inscape*.
Yet Hopkins uses the words *instress* and *inscape* in notes on
Parmenides which apparently were written about February 9,
1868, four years before he first read Scotus.[19] Therefore it
seems impossible that Scotus contributed to the formation of
his ideas of instress and inscape. Moreover, a study of the
work written on the relationship of Scotus and Hopkins shows

[17] Christopher Devlin, S. J., "Gerard Manley Hopkins and Duns Scotus,"
New Verse, XIV (1935), 12–17.
[18] *Notebooks and Papers*, p. 161.
[19] See *Journals and Papers*, p. 127.

an unexpected reason for the popularity of this topic among critics. We have seen above that Herbert Read's criticism of Hopkins was very influential in the rise of Hopkins' reputation, that Read's ideas are closely related to Hulme's distinction between intensive and extensive manifolds, which is used to defend the intuitive nature of art, and that Hulme derives his distinction between intensive and extensive manifolds from Bergson's distrust of the rational faculty. It is perhaps significant that Christopher Devlin, in the first attempt to explore the relationship of Hopkins and Duns Scotus,[20] quotes Bergson almost as much as Scotus himself. Scotus' *haecceitas*, or quality of individuation, is generally treated as an explanation of the inadequacy of the rational faculty of the human mind. The rational faculty must generalize, put things in categories, but the world is too complex for that treatment. The reason can abstract *qualitas*, but *haecceitas* remains. It seems possible that the reason critics find Scotus' idea of *haecceitas* so important is not so much because it fits Hopkins' theory of inscape but because it reinforces Bergson's theory of intuition in art which underlies Read's defense of Hopkins. If scholars following Read begin to assume that Hopkins is valuable because of the intuitive nature of his art, it is likely that they will find a philosophical system which seems to justify intuitive art, and which may have influenced Hopkins, a more congenial subject to study than other possible influences.[21]

[20] Devlin, " Gerard Manley Hopkins and Duns Scotus," pp. 12–17.

[21] Scholars have been strangely reticent to discuss Hopkins' actual references to Scotus. There are real problems in the text of Hopkins' papers: the late date of Hopkins' first reading of Scotus; the small number of direct references to Scotus; but most important of all the strange reference to Scotus in the *Sermons and Devotional Writings*, p. 151: " Is not this pitch or whatever we call it then the same as Scotus's *ecceitas?* " It is a curious error when a man with a first in classical greats mistakes *ecceitas* for *haecceitas*. The editor explains, " The Italian form of *haecceitas* is *ecceita*. Possibly Gerard Manley Hopkins derived it from Fr. le Gonidec of the Roman Province. . . . Perhaps also the association of *Ecce!* ' Look! '

The influence of the discipline of Loyola and the Society of Jesus was acknowledged early in the study of Hopkins, but at first the critics tended to concentrate on mainly biographical problems as, for example, in Pick's *Gerard Manley Hopkins: Priest and Poet*. Recently, in David A. Downes' *Gerard Manley Hopkins: A Study of his Ignatian Spirit*,[22] there has been a change in emphasis from biographical to artistic consequences of Loyola's influence on Hopkins. The study of the effect of Loyola's teaching on Hopkins' concept of art needs to be carried further. W. H. Gardner's *Gerard Manley Hopkins: A Study of Poetic Idiosyncracy in Relation to Poetic Tradition*[23] is the most thorough treatment of Hopkins as a Victorian. Gardner explores Hopkins' relationship to Newman, Pater, Ruskin; the Oxford movement, the aesthetic movement, and the Pre-Raphaelites. Arthur Mizener[24] stoutly maintains that Hopkins was less eccentric than is commonly thought and that he possesses an essentially Victorian sensibility. Austin Warren,[25] too, maintains that Hopkins learned much from Keats, the medieval school or Pre-Raphaelites, Pater, Ruskin, Newman, and the Victorian linguistic studies of Furnivall, Barnes, and others who sought to restore teutonic English. Finally, there is an unpublished doctoral

appealed to him. It is possible that he was not familiar with the word in the original, since it does not occur in the *Scriptum Oxoniense* which he seems chiefly to have read. It occurs, so far as I know, only in the *Reportata Parisiensia*, II, xii, 5." We might observe that *ecce* would be σκοπέ in Greek and σκοπέ transliterates as "scope," but such conjecture is idle. See *Further Letters*, pp. 284–85, on the etymology of *scope* and *scape*.

[22] David A. Downes, *Gerard Manley Hopkins: A Study of his Ignatian Spirit* (New York: Bookman Associates, 1959).

[23] W. H. Gardner, *Gerard Manley Hopkins: A Study of Poetic Idiosyncrasy in Relation to Poetic Tradition*, 2 vols. (New Haven: Yale University Press, 1948–1949). Also Vol. I (London: Martin Seeker and Warburg, 1944).

[24] Arthur Mizener, "Victorian Hopkins," *Gerard Manley Hopkins*, by the Kenyon Critics, pp. 94–114.

[25] Austin Warren, "Instress of Inscape," *Gerard Manley Hopkins*, by the Kenyon Critics, pp. 72–88.

dissertation by Roberta Holloway [26] which argues that Hopkins' terms *instress* and *inscape* are derived from his study of Parmenides and Heraclitus. But these studies compose only a small part of the body of criticism. There are surprisingly few attempts to relate Hopkins to his age or to find the sources of his ideas. It is far more common for a scholar to assume that Hopkins is detached from tradition than to try to demonstrate the derivation of his ideas.

Just as the critics seem to be reluctant to study the traditional element in Hopkins' ideas, so they seem to hesitate to study the traditional element in his style—with two exceptions. Hopkins' style has been most frequently compared to the "metaphysical poets" and to Whitman. Heywood [27] finds a primitive and a metaphysical strain in his verse which shows the influence of Whitman and Donne. Matthiessen [28] has perhaps the most convincing study of Whitman and Hopkins, Austin Warren [29] of Hopkins and Donne; and Phare [30] has an extended study of Hopkins and Crashaw. It is not surprising that critics should try to establish a relationship among their favorite writers, but it is possible that the main point in common among such poets as Donne, Hopkins, and Whitman is the fact that they all appeal to certain critics and that from their common appeal the critics then are led to deduce a relationship among the poets which might otherwise not be apparent. The most frequently cited bit of evidence suggesting a connection between Whitman and Hopkins is an enigmatic passage in a letter written to Bridges on October 18,

[26] Roberta Holloway, "Some Effects of Classical Study in the Work of Hopkins" (unpublished doctoral dissertation, University of California, Berkeley, 1945).

[27] Terence Heywood, "Hopkins' Ancestry," *Poetry*, LIV (1939), 209–18.

[28] F. O. Matthiessen, *American Renaissance* (New York: Oxford University Press, 1941), pp. 584–92.

[29] Warren, "Instress of Inscape," *Gerard Manley Hopkins*, by the Kenyon Critics, pp. 72–88.

[30] Phare, *Poetry*.

1882, " But first I may as well say what I should not otherwise
have said, that I always knew in my heart Walt Whitman's
mind to be more like my own than any other man's living. As
he is a very great scoundrel this is not a pleasant confession.
And this also makes me the more desirous to read him and
the more determined that I will not." [31] If this quotation is
restored to its context, however, the force of the letter as a
whole is to deny any similarity between Whitman and Hopkins' deliberate style of writing. Bridges had apparently
accused Hopkins of echoing Whitman. This letter is a refutation of that charge. First, Hopkins explains that the only
pieces by Whitman he has read are "(1) ' Pete ' in the library
at Bedford Square (and perhaps something else; if so I forget),
which you pointed out; (2) two pieces in the *Athenaeum* or
Academy, one on the Man-of-War Bird, the other beginning
' Spirit that formed this scene '; (3) short extracts in a review
by Saintsbury in the *Academy*: this is all I remember. I cannot have read more than half a dozen pieces at most." [32] Hopkins then grants that very little exposure to an artist's work
may make a lasting impression and, still playing the devil's
advocate, he grants that Whitman's mind is like his own.
Nevertheless, his argument is that he is free from a similarity
to Whitman in poetic style: " On second thoughts you will
find the fancied resemblance diminish and the imitation dis-
appear." [33] The evidence is at best equivocal.

The attention given to the alleged direct relationship of
Donne and Crashaw to Hopkins is still more surprising because it has never been established that Hopkins read a single
word by these authors. There seems to be no reference to
them in his papers. A list of all the authors Hopkins mentions
shows a heavy preponderance of Latin and Greek authors

[31] *Letters*, p. 155.   [33] *Ibid.*, p. 155.
[32] *Ibid.*, p. 154.

and modern scholars of classical languages. Theologians and religious writers make up a large part of the list, nineteenth-century British writers are rather fully represented, but English and Continental secular writers publishing before 1750 appear quite seldom. Although we have several studies of the similarities of Donne, Crashaw, and Hopkins, we have no evidence that Hopkins ever read Donne and Crashaw.

A number of writers have tried to define Hopkins' terms and ideas, such as *inscape* or *sprung rhythm*. The treatment of sprung rhythm can serve as an example of this approach. The first reaction to Hopkins' explanation of his metrics was to deny any value to his ideas, as did G. M. Young's essay on meter.[34] Among those who believe Hopkins' metrical ideas have some value, there seem to be three schools of thought. First, Harold Whitehall [35] and others maintain that Hopkins' sprung rhythm is an imperfectly executed version of Patmore's dipodic theory. Walter Ong [36] maintains that Whitehall confuses stress and timing and offers as an alternative explanation that sprung rhythm is based on the sense stress of common speech and thus eliminates the fictitious metrical norm which is a part of ordinary English verse. Gardner,[37] in perhaps the most promising treatment, attempts to explain sprung rhythm in terms of classical verse. While no single study has given the final explanation of sprung rhythm, this method of approaching Hopkins seems to be more profitable than, for example, the method used in exploring the poet-priest relationship.

Exegesis of particular poems follows a general pattern of which the criticism of " The Windhover " will give us a fair

[34] G. M. Young, " Forty Years of Verse," *London Mercury*, XXXV (1936), 112–22.

[35] Harold Whitehall, " Sprung Rhythm," *Gerard Manley Hopkins*, by the Kenyon Critics, pp. 28–55.

[36] Walter Ong, " Hopkins' Sprung Rhythm and the Life of English Poetry," *Immortal Diamond*, pp. 93–175.

[37] Gardner, *Gerard Manley Hopkins*, pp. 11, 98–137.

example. Some critics maintain that there is no allegory or symbolism in the poem.[38] Most, however, feel that there is symbolism and the explanations of it show a tendency to become more and more complex as the body of critical writing on Hopkins grows. Doubtless one of the reasons for this poem's popularity is the flexible nature of its symbolism whereby Christians read the poem as Hopkins' battle cry while anti-Christians find it a cry of despair. One group of readers maintains that the poet whose heart is hiding in the cloister cries out in admiration of the bird, which symbolizes the poet's lost freedom. A second group maintains that the word " buckle " signifies joining the Jesuits and that the poet, or perhaps Christ himself, advises man to " buckle to " and live properly, as the windhover flies bravely, for in this way man will be most beautiful in Christ's eyes. The tendency in defending either of these interpretations against the other has been to extend the symbolic meanings alleged to be found in the poem. Thus we are told that *falcon* signifies a holy man, *skate* (which is a kind of fish) stands for Christ, *plow* symbolizes the prelatical office, and *ember* stands for the passion of Christ.[39] Once we admit the existence of symbolism, there seems to be no end to the meanings suggested.

No brief summary can do justice to the really impressive body of critical writing on Hopkins. The reader must see, however, that the critical theories which led to the rise of Hopkins' reputation as a poet carried with them certain assumptions about the nature of his poetry and certain attitudes toward the poet which have influenced subsequent scholarly investigation to follow the same lines. For example, Richards' theory of psychical poise, which was instrumental in the rise of Hopkins' reputation, implies a subjective approach to the poetry whereby the critic studies the effect of the poetry on

[38] T. J. Grady, " Windhover's Meaning," *America*, VII (1944), 465–66.
[39] R. W. Ayers, " Hopkins' ' The Windhover,' a Further Simplification," pp. 577–84.

the mind of the reader, rather than the mind of the author. This approach is quite apparent in the critical writings subsequent to Richards. Likewise, Read's praise of organic form, which supplied the justification for Hopkins' oddity, implies that Hopkins was detached from literary tradition. Despite valuable work by Gardner, Warren, Mizener, Downes, and others, the image persists of Hopkins as a revolutionary, so detached from literary tradition that he himself did not realize the extent of his innovations. This assumption, as we shall see, can be maintained only at the expense of maintaining that the only literary tradition in lyric poetry is exemplified in Tennyson. The belief that Hopkins was naïve in literary matters deserves closer examination than it has, as yet, received.

One reason for the growth of the notion that Hopkins is isolated from any significant literary tradition is that there is no reliable biographical study of him. The amount of critical writing about Hopkins since the first edition of his poems in 1918 has been staggering. By my count, in the past forty-five years well over 700 separate articles and books give serious attention to Hopkins and, of course, many of these consider isolated biographical problems or refer to such problems by implication in dealing with his poetry. Nevertheless, of all these only two works set out primarily and systematically to present biography. (The recent study by Ritz, *Le poète Gérard Manley Hopkins*, serves to confirm, rather than contradict, the existence of an acute biographical problem in the study of Hopkins.) The first of these is Father Lahey's memoir, *Gerard Manley Hopkins*, published in London in 1930, the year of the second edition of the *Poems*. Although Lahey's biography was the first book devoted entirely to Hopkins, it is only 172 pages long and was written before the papers and letters of Hopkins had been edited for publication. The value of Lahey's work resided in its priority, not its dependability. The second attempt at pure biography is Eleanor Ruggles' *Gerard Manley Hopkins, A Life*, published in New York in 1944. It is a fictionalized account, possibly of some value as light reading, but of little interest otherwise.

Considering the apparent deficiencies of these studies, why have there been no further attempts? What unusual problems drive the student into textual rather than biographical criticism? First, of course, there is the curious dual context in which Hopkins exists. He had been dead nearly thirty years before Robert Bridges issued the first edition of his work. He therefore wrote and lived in one generation, and was read only in another. And so, when his work appeared, his admirers in the postwar years could observe directly the complexities of the texture of his verse but not the complexities of his life. Moreover, the first edition of the poems by Bridges in 1918 could hardly be called immediately successful. Not until the crucial article by Richards in *The Dial* in 1926 did a strong current of critical opinion favorable to Hopkins begin to flow. But the critics who were most favorably disposed toward Hopkins in the 1920's and 30's had certain assumptions about the nature of art that are uncongenial to biographical or historical study. They wanted art to possess organic form, the artist therefore to be in rebellion against established form. These critics wanted to see Hopkins as detached from corrupt Victorian poetic idiom. Such an attitude hardly encourages the biographical study of a writer who so undeniably lived under the reign of Victoria. But in addition to all these special problems, there is still another discouragement for the biographer. If we put Lahey's memoir or Ruggles' life beside the published letters and notes of Hopkins, the secondary studies are overwhelmed by the primary sources. The published papers demonstrate in a direct and forceful prose such subtle variety, such depth of mind that the scholar may well despair of finding any other presentation adequate for the man.

In six stout volumes, fragments of Hopkins' own corre-spondence and notes stand as the one main source of infor-mation about him. Claude Colleer Abbott's editions of the letters to Robert Bridges and the correspondence with Richard Watson Dixon present a curious three-cornered game of intellectual catch among the Jesuit professor of classics, the anti-Catholic physician, and the Canon of the Church of England—serious poets all three. Here in the first criticism of Hopkins' "Deutschland," or Bridges' "Eros and Psyche," or Dixon's "Christ's Company" the tensions between the unique personal genius of each man and the general intellectual movements of his time appear more vividly than any biog-rapher could hope to depict them. So, too, in the case of Humphrey House's edition of *The Notebooks and Papers of Gerard Manley Hopkins* in 1937 (recently reissued in an ex-panded form as *The Journals and Papers of Gerard Manley Hopkins*), how can the scholar adequately represent the minute and intricate patterns of his natural description, the keen logical analysis which is evident even in his undergradu-ate themes, or his fascination with the structure and function of language expressed in the elaborate philological notes. Al-most every page supplies an example of his distinctive observa-tions about the etymologies and linguistic connections between various words. Hopkins says, for example, about the word *horn* in English,

"From the shape, *kernel* and *granum*, *grain*, corn. From the curve of a horn, *koronis*, *corona*, *crown*. From the spiral *crinis*, meaning ringlets, locks. From its being the highest point comes our *crown* perhaps, in the sense of the top of the head, and the Greek *keras*, horn, and *kara*, head, were evi-dently identical; then for its sprouting up and growing, compare *keren*, *cornu*, *keras*, horn with grow, *cresco*, *grandis*, grass, great, *groot*. For its curving, *curvus* is probably from the root horn in one of its forms. *Korone* in Greek and *corvus*, *cornix* in Latin and *crow* (perhaps also *raven*, which may have been *craven* originally) in English bear a striking resemblance to *cornu, curvus*. So also *Geranos, crane, heron, herne*. Why these birds should derive their names from *horn* I cannot presume to say." [40]

How can a biographer go about describing this characteristic preoccupation with linguistic connections in sound, root, function, and etymology of words except by quoting examples from the author's own hand?

Abbott continued his editorial work in 1938 with *The Further Letters of Gerard Manley Hopkins* including the personal letters telling the story of his conversion to the Roman Catholic faith and the painful alienation from his family which followed that spiritual crisis. More recently, in 1959 Christopher Devlin edited *The Sermons and Devotional Writings* including, on the one hand, those strangely convoluted and moving sermons tending toward overelaboration like so many baroque emblems and, on the other hand, the lucid commentary on *The Spiritual Exercises* of Ignatius and other theological texts.

These six volumes of fragmentary prose served to consolidate Hopkins' literary reputation perhaps as much as the poetry itself. The papers appeal to readers in two ways: they tell the story of Hopkins' intense intellectual drama and at the same time reveal his acute critical mind at work. For example, Harris Downey's review of the first two volumes of letters in *The Virginia Quarterly Review*, 1935, is typical of the response to Hopkins' prose. He asserts that these books will add to Hopkins' stature because, first, they delineate " the drama born of a mind wherein opposing factors constantly arise and are constantly resolved. The opposition is provoked not by externality—the world of men, machines, and chauvinisms—but by contrary desires of a mind that turned its observation inward to investigate itself " (pp. 458–61). But in addition to this biographical interest, there is the equally im-

[40] *Notebooks and Papers*, p. 5.

portant literary analysis. Downey continues: "The other aspect of the books is, of course, one of literary criticism. In an age almost stifled with literary history repeating itself in countless volumes and with defensive arguments that resolve themselves through casuistries to lose the paths of their amenable intents, the keen observation of an unbiased mind comes with a freshness that brings excitation to those who have wearied of the repeated failures."

Hopkins' treatment of the first line of Bridges' "Prometheus the Firegiver" demonstrates this "keen observation of an unbiased mind" that Downey praises. Bridges' line reads,

> From high Olympus and the domeless courts,
> Where mighty Zeus our angry king confirms
> The Fates' decrees and bends the will of the gods,
> I come.

In a letter to Bridges, Hopkins protests:

> Nothing can reconcile me to "domeless." . . . It has two independent faults, either of which would condemn it: courts are uncovered spaces in their nature; all then are roofless, *a fortiori* domeless; so that the word is without point. And next domes were not used by the Greeks, the keepings of whose art and architecture you are to keep to: so then again of course the buildings of Olympus, let alone the courts, are domeless. And there remains an infelicity still. For when anything, as a court, is uncovered and roofless strictly speaking, a dome is just the one kind of roof it may still be said to have and especially in a clear sky and on a mountain, namely the spherical vault or dome of heaven. What *can* you say?
>
> P.S. And I may even add that *domeless* is a heavy sinking-rhythm word here. You want a lifting word—aerial.[41]

Bridges emended the word to *aetherial*.

Until the publication of Antony Bischoff's projected biography of Hopkins, the student of his verse will depend almost entirely upon his published prose as a source of information

[41] *Letters*, p. 243.

about the man and these papers will, in any case, stand as intrinsically valuable literary criticism demonstrating surprisingly modern techniques of close reading and analysis. It is a great pity, therefore, that these published notes represent only a fragment of his papers. In his article in *Thought* (Winter, 1951) Bischoff has told the sad tale of the dispersal of Hopkins' files which makes, as he observes, " difficult, if not impossible any final evaluation of Hopkins' genius." But, mainly through Bischoff's efforts, a large number of unpublished papers have been recovered and collected at the library of Campion Hall at Oxford.

Among these papers as yet unpublished there is one group of seven manuscripts which, considered together, call for a modification in the prevailing view of Hopkins. The notebook designated in Bischoff's Catalog as C II, 137 leaves, some mutilated, dated on the verso of the flyleaf May 23, 1862, contains detailed notes on Thucydides, *Prometheus Desmotes*, the *Khoephoroi*, *Agamemnon*, *Eumenides*, *Ajax*, and *Oedipus Rex*, as well as a few disconnected notes on history. The notes on Thucydides and perhaps Prometheus seem to date from Hopkins' school days at Highgate; notes on the other plays are perhaps college work including Riddell's and Jowett's readings of various passages. Notebook M II contains 85 pages of textual and other comments on the *Nicomachian Ethics*, probably undergraduate work; M III, 71 pages of notes on *Seven Against Thebes*; M IV, notes headed " Metrical etc. —notes made at Stonyhurst "; M V, detailed notes on Books 4, 5, and 6 of the *Iliad* which fit in with marginalia in Hopkins' copy of Homer. The notes on Homer seem to have been used by Hopkins in teaching or lecturing when he was professor of Greek at University College, Dublin. Notebooks G II and G III (sometimes called the Dublin notebook) contain personal memoranda and lecture notes for Roman literature and antiquities dated 1888 in the text. All of these unpublished papers show Hopkins at work as a scholar of classical literature.

Although there is a tendency to see Hopkins as so naïve in literary matters that he was not even conscious of his art, most critics agree that there is a connection between his peculiar style of writing poetry and the substance of his published notes. It is only a step from the frequent philological entries supplying sometimes fanciful connections between series of words such as " Drill, trill, thrill, nostril, nese-thril " or " Flick, fillip, flip, fleck, flake " [42] to the characteristic verbal intoxication of the first lines of such a poem as " Spelt from Sibyl's Leaves ":

> Earnest, earthless, equal, attunable ˈvaulty, voluminous, . . . stupendous
> Evening strains to be tíme's vást, ˈwomb-of-all, home-of-all, hearse-of-all night.

In a similar manner, the critical approach which Hopkins demonstrates in attacking Bridges' unfortunate *domeless courts* represents a characteristic way of reading, to use Hopkins' own word for it, a demand that each word *tell*, which seems to foresee the practice of the New Critics. If Hopkins' style of writing seems radically different from Bridges', one reason may be that he would not tolerate diction which does not *tell*. Anyone who reads Hopkins' criticism will see that he would have observed the horrible truth about Joyce Kilmer's " Trees " just as effectively as Brooks and Warren. He has a sure eye for mixed metaphor, imprecise connotation or denotation, and dead phrases.

But was Hopkins' intense concern for etymological resonances of words and his habit of close reading of poetry as intuitive as is generally believed, or was it learned? To answer this question, we should turn to his school work. As he prepared for his first examinations, or " moderations," in classi-

---

[42] *Journals and Papers*, pp. 10–11.

cal greats in school and college he would practice writing Latin and Greek prose and specified meters, and he would read set texts in the learned languages for his final, or "honours," examination. The unpublished MS C II is an example of his work during his last days in school and his first terms at Oxford.

These notes are not necessarily original work. On folio 58v Hopkins says, " The following notes were taken down when reading the play with Mr. Chavasse in Riddell's absence, and have not Riddell's authority." They are of interest precisely for this reason. Here we have a record of Hopkins' method of study. With meticulous care he would write out these notes in pencil and then revise them in ink, tracing over the pencil marks with a pen directly, apparently erasing some notes and rewriting them in ink. Such care would indicate that he considered this work extremely important.

MS C II begins with some misplaced notes on *Prometheus Desmotes*, but the earliest work in it appears to be Hopkins' commentary on Thucydides beginning with Book II, line 87. Here we have an extended example of what Hopkins learned to do in school. The first note of some length occurs on folio 3r and treats the maneuver of the Athenian ships described in Thucydides Book II, line 90. It shows how Hopkins had been taught to read a text. The entire note, including two maps which Hopkins drew to illustrate his explanation, is reproduced here:

> ἔπλεον ἐπὶ τὴν ἑαυτῶν γῆν ἔσω ἐπὶ τοῦ κόλπου *rowed upon their own land inwards in the direction of the gulf*, where *upon* is in the sense of military expression "the advanced guard will move upon Quatre-bras" *i.e.* towards it as its destination, and *their own land* means Peloponnesus, the Peloponnesians being the subject of the whole sentence, (this is given by Shepherd and Evans in their notes on Thucydides I, II; or *rowed towards their own (i.e. the Athenians) land*, where ἑαυτῶν refers to the Athenians who were possessed of Nau-

paktia to which *their own land* refers. (This is Grote's reading.) The passage has occasioned immense discussion. The Scholiast says ἐπὶ is here used for παρά. This is rejected universally and I think with perfect reason. Arnold rather gives it "a mixed signification of motion towards a place, and neighbourhood to it; expressing that the Peloponnesians sailed towards their own land, (i. e. towards Corinth, Siegon, and Pellene, to which places the greater number of the ships belonged; * *) instead of standing over to the opposite coast, which belonged to their enemies; and at the same time kept close *upon* their own land, in the sense of ἐπὶ with a dative case." If ἑαυτῶν γῆν means the Peloponnese at all the words ἔσω ἐπὶ τοῦ κόλπου sufficiently indicate that they sailed "towards Corinth, Siegon, and Pellene" without explaining that "the greater number of the ships belonged" to these places. But I think this "mixed signification" of ἐπὶ impossible. Shepherd and Evans think that Arnold has weakened his own cause but is in the right; they cannot believe in Grote's rendering of ἑαυτῶν γῆν and suggest *upon* ἐπὶ, in the military sense-*Vide Supra*. They point out, perhaps with perfect truth, that a squadron, weighing anchor from Panormos, might appear to be standing for Naupaktos when in reality it was merely intending to double the projecting point of the Peloponnese which forms the Eastern horn of Panormos, (they mean the promontory of Drepanon;) they wished to make the Athenians suppose they were meditating an attack on Naupaktos; and Thucydides, writing accurately, will not say that they were standing for Naupaktos, but, knowing the shape of the coast, describes them as moving *upon* their own land, in particular the promontory of Drepanon. This is ingenious but I believe firmly quite untenable. (I have developed their argument in the fairest and strongest way I can.) Grote, judging by common sense and the necessities of the case, makes τὴν ἑαυτῶν γῆν refer to Naupaktia; but when he says that it *hardly could* refer to the Peloponnese because *their own land* would not be within the Crissaian gulf to the western allies of Lakedaimon, I think he is hypercritical, and is confused by the words ἔσω ἐπὶ τοῦ κόλπου. For, the armament being called that of the Peloponnesians, the words τὴν ἑαυτῶν γῆν might, if other considerations permitted, be applied with perfect fitness to the whole Peloponnese, while ἔσω ἐπὶ τοῦ κόλπου marks that they were making for that part which lay within or at the extremity of the gulf. Again when Shepherd and Evans answer that *their own land*, as applied to an armament moving towards one particular part not common to all that armament, is no looser, than the same term applied to northern Greece because Attica was in it, they shew mere ignorance in not being aware that, if it can apply to northern Greece at all, it means the territory round Naupaktos which was a station of the Athenians'. The point is, can it be shewn that it is possible for *their own land* to mean, as at a *prima facie* view it would, the Peloponnese. Grote thinks not, and to justify his version of it as referring to the Athenians, he quotes parallel passages. Messrs. S. and E. think these do not prove his point. I cannot enter into this point; but I think that if it can be shewn that *their own land* must, from topographical etc. reason, mean Naupaktos, the questions will be decided by the logic of facts in favour of Grote. The strongest argument in my mind against him is the silence of the Scholiast on the possibility of *their own land* meaning anything but the Peloponnese; it evidently never entered his head that it could refer to Naupaktia. However it may be that this arises not from the grammatical impossibility of *their own land* referring to the Athenians, but from the Scholiast, ignorant of the geography of the case, not having had reason to look in that direction for a solution of the difficulty of the passage. The passage in full is as follows:

οἱ δὲ Πελοποννήσιοι, ἐπειδὴ αὐτοῖς οἱ Ἀθηναῖοι οὐκ ἐπέπλεον ἐς τὸν κόλπον καὶ τὰ στενά, βουλόμενοι ἄκοντας ἔσω προαγαγεῖν αὐτούς, ἀναγαγόμενοι ἅμα ἕῳ ἔπλεον, ἐπὶ τεσσάρων ταξάμενοι τὰς ναῦς, παρὰ τὴν ἑαυτῶν γῆν ἔσω ἐπὶ τοῦ κόλπου.

But to proceed to the refutation of S and E.

I. To translate ἐπὶ (with the accusative) *upon* in the military sense is ingenious, but without authority. Besides what an obscure and extraordinary phrase to use with the words which follow. Surely Thucydides, had he meant this, would have said *towards the promontory of Drepanon* or something of the kind.

before the Engagement.

NAUPAKTIA (ATHENIAN TERRITORY)

NAUPAKTOS (Colonized with Messenians, but then garrison.)

AITOLIA

Makunei

Tomb of Nessos.

MOLUKRIA (friendly ans) · MOLUKREION to the Athenians

The Molukrik Rhion (i.e. the Nize of Molukria), or Antirrhion.

The Akhaïk Rhion (i.e. the Nize of Akhaïa), or Rhion (i.e. the Naze)

KRISAIAN, KRISSAIAN or KRESSAIAN GULF. Drepanon (= Sickle)

PANORMOS

Temple of Athene

AKHAÏA

Temple of Poseidon

MAP A

PLATE I

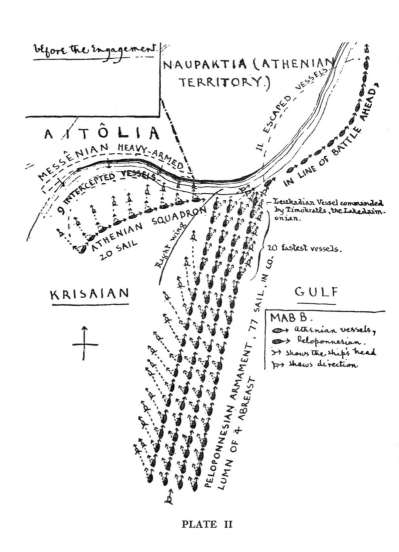

before the Engagement.

NAUPAKTIA (ATHENIAN TERRITORY.)

AITÔLIA

MESSENIAN HEAVY-ARMED

9 INTERCEPTED VESSELS

ATHENIAN SQUADRON 20 SAIL

Right wing

IL ESCAPED VESSELS

IN LINE OF BATTLE AHEAD.

—Leukadian Vessel commanded by Timokratês, the Lakedaimonian.

20 fastest vessels.

KRISAIAN

GULF

PELOPONNESIAN ARMAMENT, 77 SAIL IN COLUMN OF 4 ABREAST

MAB B.
⟨⟨⟩⟩→ Athenian vessels,
⟩→ Peloponnesian.
⟩→ shows the ship's head
⟩→ shows direction

PLATE II

II. It happens that there *is* a peculiar conformation of coast which renders this reading *possible*, and by which vessels standing for the promontory of Drepanon from Panormos might appear to be standing for Naupaktos or *vice versa*. But was Thucydides aware of this? And even supposing him either by personal observation or by careful and accurate description to have known it, surely it is the last degree of improbability that he would, using terms which when the exact features of the case were known would prove to be applicable but without this knowledge be likely to lead them astray, have his readers to conjecture his meaning without a clue? I think rather he would have carefully have explained the peculiarities of the case. I think then that one of the two following hypotheses must explain this passage.

I. τὴν ἑαυτῶν γῆν means Naupaktia and Grote is entirely in the right. ἑαυτῶν refers to the Athenians and is to be explained by supposing Thucydides' meaning fully to have been *the Peloponnesians, wishing to draw the unwilling Athenians into the gulf, thought that, an attack being made* on Naupaktos, the Athenians would be compelled to defend *their own possessions*. The word ἑαυτῶν would not generally be used, but here it is influenced by αὐτοὺς a little before and assumes an unusual meaning.

II. Thucydides supposed Naupaktos to be farther within the Crissaian gulf than it really does. The Peloponnesians therefore put out from Panormos and stood for that part of their own land, the Peloponnese, which lay within the gulf, that is to the east; they intended as actually happened, that the Athenians should suspect them to be preparing an attack of Naupaktos which lay also to the east, though on the other side of the gulf to the Peloponnese. There is no doubt that the Peloponnesians stood for Naupaktos; whether they intended actually to attack it we do not know, but it was undefended (ἐρήμῳ). The object of the Peloponnesians was attained if the Athenians supposed them to be about to do so and came to its assistance. Hence Grote's explanation agrees admirably with the facts of the case, but it is doubtful if it is grammatical. I saw today (June 16th) a passage in Herodotus I. which is almost exactly parallel to this in the

use of the αὐτὸς and ἑαυτοῦ which I must say told much
against Grote. It may be after all, that, although Shepherd
and Evans are wrong (as I am sure they are) about *upon*,
yet Thucydides might have meant something of the kind,
and might have explained himself thus. "The Peloponnesians
put out from Panormos in the direction of home. To the
ordinary reader it would appear from what follows that
Naupaktos lies in such a position that the Athenians might
very reasonably suppose the Peloponnesians about to attack
it. Perhaps he might suppose that the Peloponnesians advanced E down the Crissaian gulf and thus were in a position
to attack Naupaktos by steering to port. But the real fact
is that Napaktos lies only a point or so E. of N. with regard
to Panormos, and that the Peloponnesian fleet in steering for
Corinth etc. must stand for the N. in order to weather Cape
Drepanon, because that promontory lies on the east side
of Panormos and extends northwards. But it was unnecessary
to explain this. A reader on the spot would know how
exactly to take the words, while other readers would understand the battle and the manoeuvres equally well without
this by taking the words of the narrative as appeared
natural." It is right to say that some of the manuscripts do
read παρὰ for ἐπὶ and of these three, and another besides,
omit ἑαυτῶν. An account of the battle will be given presently.

We must remember that these notes on Thucydides are the
work of a schoolboy and written on an assigned text. Yet
when this work is compared to any criticism of English texts
written by Hopkins at the same age, for example his notes
on Tennyson's "Vision of Sin" in his letter to E. H. Coleridge dated September 3, 1862, it is the notes on Thucydides
which resemble more the mature criticism that appeals to
critics as "the keen observation of an unbiased mind." It
seems clear that Hopkins *learned* to read systematically, that
his early criticism of English is much more vague, much more
prone to accept the stock response or to pass over ambiguities
than is his criticism of Latin and Greek texts. In other words,

he learned to read carefully in his assigned school work before he applied the same rigor to his reading of English poetry.

In MS C II the notes on Thucydides are sandwiched between notes on *Prometheus Desmotes*. Hopkins begins with a discussion of the dramatis personae. Kratos is Might, the impersonation of the power of Zeus. Bia is Violence and may be considered the active part of the principle of which Kratos is the passive. Then Hopkins passes on to an analysis of obscure words and phrases: for example, the word *dios* at line 88 calls for a note which we see typical of Hopkins' later papers, " *Dyaus* in Sanscrit is the *open sky*, whence *deus, divus, dius, dies,* Zeus, Διός, δῖος, θεός, θεῦος also *Ju*-piter, *Dies*-piter, *Dis, Jovis*; Sanscrit *Deva*, (*god.*)" The point of such a note on a classical text is to build up the connotations of a word for a student who does not know the language thoroughly enough to grasp the full resonance of the diction without help. It is, of course, quite similar in its effects to Empson's study of the function of complex words.

We can open this notebook practically at random and find evidence that Hopkins *learned* to read closely, that the curriculum of classical greats taught him to approach a text in a certain way. In *The Khoephoroi* of Aeschylus, at line 177, Electra mourns, " I am struck through, as by the cross stab of a sword, and from my eyes the thirsty and unguarded drops burst in a storm of tears like winter rain." One problem with this metaphor is that the adjective δίψιοι, *thirsty*, modifies σταγόνες, *raindrops*. Hopkins comments:

> 177. δίψιοι as an epithet of σταγόνες is a difficult word. It is one of those poetical touches which cannot be reduced to exact explanation but convey a fine image nevertheless. It *may* mean *eager*, or else perhaps *thirsty* is put for *thirstily-drunk* as the first large drops of a thunder shower would be. I would try *salt* in something of the same sense: because salt excites thirst. The Editors of course proceed to arrive at the sense by the method Aristophanes describes as used by

Dionusos in Hades, weighing tragedy by ounce and scruple, and measuring it with squares, yard-measures, etc.

In short, Hopkins observed δίψιοι in Greek *tells* whereas *thirsty* in English does not.

We might well note his comment on line 1457 and those following in the *Agamemnon* of Aeschylus, which reads in Greek: " ἦ μέγαν οἴκοις τοῖσδε δαίμονα καὶ βαρύμηνιν αἰνεῖς φεῦ, φεῦ, κακὸν αἶνον ἀτηρᾶς τύχας ἀκορέστομ ἰώ, ἰή, διαὶ Διὸς παναιτίου, πανεργέτα." Hopkins observes, " 1457–1465, curious alliterations and assonances, which have not been sufficiently noticed in Greek tragedy, are here indulged in (correspondences in words, etc.), αἰνεῖς, αἶνον— ἰώ, ἰή, διαὶ Διὸς (line 1461)—παναιτίου, πανεργέτα (line 1462)—πελεῖται, τί τῶν δ'." One of the main characteristics of Hopkins' English verse, of course, is just such alliteration and assonance.

Among the earliest of the loose notes apparently from his school days there is a list of rhetorical devices, anacoluthon, oxymoron, asyndeton, and so on, each illustrated by examples in Latin, Greek, and English. From this elementary beginning we can follow the development of Hopkins' sophistication as a reader until he customarily comments on the function of rhetorical devices in their context, as, for example, his comment on *The Choephoroi*:

> 725. θέτο; Paley substitutes ἔθετο, but I think that the whole speech is purposely ungrammatical etc. to suit the character of the nurse:—a rare point with Aeschylus who seems to be of Puff's opinion—"Sneer. But, Mr. Puff, I think not only the Justice, but the clown seems to talk in as high a style as the first here among them. Puff. Heaven forbid they should not, in a free country! Sir, I am not for making slavish distinctions, and giving all the fine language to the upper sort of people": witness the monstrous anacoluthon in 745–47, the probable one in 736 et. seq., the clumsy sentence in 724–28, in 738–41, the phrase εὖτ' ἄν πύθηται and the line 743: θέτο then is probably an old-fashioned country form.

Such a comment shows that Hopkins learned from his assigned study of Latin and Greek that a distortion in language represents an imitation of the way the mind of a particular speaker works. So, too, in this same notebook we can observe where Hopkins jotted down the names of the common metrical feet with diagrammatic illustrations of each, the spondee, pyrrhic, iambus, trochee, dactyl, cretic, anapaest, bacchius, amphibrachus, molossus, and so on. From this introduction of classical metrics, he progresses rapidly to the analysis of dramatic choruses and speculation about the effects of various irregularities and variations (especially in Ms M III, notes on *Seven against Thebes*).

In these papers Hopkins demonstrates his developing techniques as a reader. Specifically, he examines the etymology of each important word; he identifies the rhetorical device in which the word is used; he determines the denotation of the word and what it tells the reader about the speaker; he examines the metrical structure looking for meaningful relationships of sounds; in short, he practices all the techniques of close reading in his study of Latin and Greek that reviewers have found so refreshing in his criticism of English poetry. When we put all of the existing papers in chronological order, it appears that Hopkins' sophistication as a reader developed first in his school work.

The tendency to consider Hopkins naïve in literary matters originated with critics who admire organic form and who, therefore, want to see him as a rebel against all existing discipline. Because we have no adequate biography of Hopkins as yet, his published papers stand as the main source of information about him and encourage the tendency to treat him as detached from all literary tradition because his critical voice, like his poetic voice, "seems to come out of the blue, reminding us of nothing we have heard before," as C. Day Lewis says. Yet these published papers omit Hopkins' school work and his adult lecture and study notes on classical texts because they seem to be of no interest. Doubtless these papers do lack the drama of Hopkins' personal correspondence, but we must nevertheless turn to them if we wish to see Hopkins at work, to see the development of his critical faculty. Of course, only a man of great individual genius would respond to his studies so sensitively and so originally. But we do not deny his brilliance as an innovator when we observe simply that Hopkins' education trained him to read and his method of reading was an important influence on his style of writing. The critics who fostered the idea of Hopkins' intellectual detachment were themselves not disinterested, but had an intense commitment to the idea that all great poets are essentially rebels.

Although the rise of Hopkins' reputation after World War I depended on the aesthetic theories of Richards and Read, these ideas were not totally unforeseen nor even really new. As we have seen, their line of descent stretches back through Hulme and Bergson at least to Vico. Moreover, the assumptions which led to the aesthetic theories of Richards and Read were so widespread in Victorian England that often we find the new psychological criticism written between the wars echoing, almost word for word, critical doctrines set forth a century earlier. The similarity between Macauley and Read, Vico and Richards, suggests some pervasive critical movement impelled by a consistent motive which culminates in the writing of those who praised Hopkins most vigorously.

When Read edited the works of Hulme in 1924, he found there a refinement of Bergson's idea of knowledge which is fundamental to Read's own aesthetic theory. Hulme says, " Then, the general idea behind Bergson's work: It is an endeavor to prove that we seem inevitably to arrive at the mechanistic theory [of the universe] simply because the intellect, in dealing with a certain aspect of reality, distorts it in that direction." [43] But it is precisely here that the twentieth century is most clearly the heir of the nineteenth. As Robert Langbaum in *The Poetry of Experience* has said, the growing distrust of the reflective faculty of the mind, the belief in "the doctrine that the imaginative apprehension gained through immediate experience is primary and certain, whereas the analytic reflection that follows is secondary and problematical," [44] connects the art of the twentieth century with the art of the nineteenth.

Probably one of the main causes for a growing distrust in the reflective faculty was the tendency in the popular physical science of the Victorian period to distinguish between the sensations, or impressions we have, and the physical stimuli which cause those sensations. For example, Hermann Ludwig Ferdinand von Helmholtz, whose lectures "On the Relation of Optics to Painting" supply a scientific basis for some of the techniques of French impressionistic painting, says in his essay "Harmony in Music," in 1873:

> When the siren is turned slowly, and hence the puffs of air succeed each other slowly, you hear no musical sound. By the continually increasing rapidity of its revolution, no essential change is produced in the kind of vibration of the air. Nothing new happens externally to the ear. The only new result is the sensation experienced by the ear, which then for the first time begins to be affected by the agitation of the air. Hence the more rapid vibrations receive a new name, and are called Sound. If you admire paradoxes, you may say that aerial vibrations do not become sound until they fall upon a hearing ear.[45]

The important thing to notice in this passage is that Helmholtz apparently proves scientifically that the sensation of

[43] Hulme, *Speculations*, p. 174.
[44] Robert Langbaum, *The Poetry of Experience* (London: Chatto & Windus, 1957), p. 35.
[45] H. Helmholtz, *Popular Lectures on Scientific Subjects*, 2 vols., trans. E. Atkinson (New York: Appleton Co., 1881), Vol. I, p. 70.

sound is quite different from what is " really " there, the wave which stimulates the impression of sound. In the same manner in his essay " On the Relation of Optics to Painting " he asserts that the object of the artist is to evoke the impression, not necessarily to imitate the stimuli. Therefore we must study the nature of the impression in the perceiving intellect: " The physiological study of the manner in which the perceptions of our senses originate, how impressions from without pass into our nerves, and how the condition of the latter is thereby altered, presents many points of contact with the theory of the fine arts." [46] And so the artist may be able to reproduce the sensation or impression by creating a stimulus quite different from the natural one, the subject of his painting: " The more immediate object of the painter is to produce in us by his palette a lively visual impression of the objects which he has endeavoured to represent. The aim, in a certain sense, is to produce a kind of optical illusion." [47] Although I have found no evidence that Hopkins knew the lectures of Helmholtz, Hopkins worked at writing an account of the propagation of light. He wrote to Dixon on August 7, 1886, thirteen years after the publication of Helmholtz's essay quoted above:

> I am writing (but I am almost sure I never shall have written) a sort of popular account of Light and Ether. Popular is note quite the word; it is not meant to be easy reading, for such a difficult subject can only be made easy by a very summary and sketchy treatment; rather it is meant for the lay or unprofessional student who will read carefully. . . . No such account exists and scientific books, especially in English, are very unsatisfactory.[48]

The phrase, " especially in English " might possibly suggest that he knew Helmholtz; but, in any case, he sees the infer-

[46] *Ibid.*, p. 74.
[47] *Ibid.*, p. 75.
[48] *Correspondence*, p. 139.

ence to be drawn from the apparent distinction between the impression received and its stimulus which Helmholtz delineated:

> The study of physical science has, unless corrected in some way, an effect the very opposite of what one would suppose. One would think it might materialize people (no doubt it does make them or, rather I should say, they become materialists; but this is not the same thing: they do not believe in Matter more but in God less); but in fact they seem to end in conceiving only of a world of formulas, with its being properly speaking in thought, towards which the outer world acts as a sort of feeder.[49]

As Hopkins says, the effect of the distinction between the sensation of light and the physical propagation of light tends to create doubt as to the nature of the " real " world.

We have only to look to our own ideas to see how pervasive this notion is. Every modern reader " knows " that this solid, plane page at which he is now gazing is " really " composed of separate atoms in motion with spaces between them— it is only the coarseness of his sense of sight which tricks him into supposing for a minute that the page is " really " solid, but we " know " better. This unsettling observation is not unique to the twentieth century. Walter Pater, in his conclusion to *The Renaissance*, says, " It is only the roughness of the eye that makes any two persons, things, situations, seem alike." We have inherited a dual problem: how to deal with a world in which analytic reflection is only secondary and problematical and in which our senses themselves manifestly reduce or distort the world according to their own degrees of coarseness.

Pater, who we must remember was Hopkins' tutor at Oxford in 1865, summarizes the problem in the conclusion to *The Renaissance*,

[49] *Ibid.*

At first sight experience seems to bury us under a flood of external objects. . . . But when reflection begins to play upon those objects they are dissipated under its influence; the cohesive force seems suspended like a trick of magic; each object is loosed into a group of impressions—color, odor, texture—in the mind of the observer. And if we continue to dwell in thought on this world, not of objects in the solidity with which language invests them, but of impressions, unstable, flickering, inconsistent, which burn and are extinguished with our consciousness of them, it contracts still further: the whole scope of observation is dwarfed to the narrow chamber of the individual mind. Experience, already reduced to a swarm of impressions, is ringed round for each one of us by a thick wall of personality through which no real voice has ever pierced on its way to us, or from us to that which we can only conjecture to be without. Every one of those impressions is the impression of the individual in his isolation, each mind keeping as a solitary prisoner its own dream of a world.

Hopkins' undergraduate essay, " The Probable Future of Metaphysics," written during the Hilary Term of 1867, shows how thoroughly he had accepted the idea that sensory impressions are not necessarily an accurate report of the objective world. We find him saying, for example,

Material explanation cannot be refined into explaining thought and it is all to no purpose to show an organ for each faculty and a nerve vibrating for each idea, because this only shows in the last detail what broadly no one doubted, to wit that the activities of the spirit are conveyed in those of the body as scent is conveyed in spirits of wine, remaining still inexplicably distinct. Indeed it would be necessary first in the material world to resolve force and matter into one thing and then afterwards to approach that which to all appearance alone has the power of disposing force itself, that is mind, and subsume that too under the head of the material.[50]

In short, Hopkins assumes that our mental activity is distinct from the material world and that the nature of the relationship

[50] *Journals and Papers*, p. 118.

between sensory impressions and objective reality cannot be explained. We have no way of knowing what is " really " outside the mind.

There is, in general, one common response to this growing fear. If we can trust neither the senses nor the rational faculty, there is still one fundamental fact of which we can be sure: the mind does function; *je pense*. The only verifiable thing in the world is that the mind works and, by analogy, so may other minds in a somewhat similar fashion. We can never be sure of the conclusions which the mind reaches but we can be sure of its activity. And so, as doubt in the senses and the rational faculty grows, writers turn their attention more and more to the mental activity itself. Hulme, as quoted above, uses the commonplace method to solve his dilemma when he turns to the function of the mind for evidence that the rational faculty is not adequate to deal with things as they " really " are. He finds there in the flow of mental activity what he calls an intensive manifold. It is something which we know, but which we cannot analyze. The mental activity itself is verifiable, but we know it intuitively and not through the faulty rational faculty. So, too, Pater turns to the activity of the mind as the only reality. His advice in the conclusion of *The Renaissance* to " get as many pulsations as possible into a given time," or " to burn always with this hard, gemlike flame, to maintain this ecstasy is success in life," makes sense only as a solution to the dilemma a man must reach who can trust neither his senses nor his reason. For Pater, the only verifiable thing in the world is that the mind works; therefore it is best for it to work as intensely as possible. Doubt in our ability to know the " real " world drives Hopkins to a great deal of trouble to find a new definition of beauty in his dialogue, " On The Origin of Beauty ": " Beauty therefore is a relation, and the apprehension of it a comparison. The sense of beauty in fact is a comparison, is it not? " [51] He is

[51] *Ibid.*, p. 951.

apparently eager to establish that beauty need not be understood as a form (which must be embodied in the physical world), but that it may be considered as a relation (which can exist only in a perceiving intellect). Like Pater, he believes that only the activity of the mind is verifiable. He feels therefore that he can profitably discuss the nature of beauty as a mental activity, but not as a quality of the material world about which his rational intellect can only speculate.

As doubt of the ability of the mind to deal with the external world becomes more confirmed, the poet, like the philosopher or painter, turns his attention to the mental activity itself. The center of interest in his poem shifts from the subject discussed to the activity of the intellect which perceives that subject, from what is seen to how it is seen by a particular mind. So in Browning's monologues the reader's attention shifts from what the speaker sees about him to the way the mind of the speaker works in the poem. In nineteenth-century poetry there is a distinctive movement away from interest in the nominal subject of a poem and toward an interest in the peculiar way the speaker sees that subject. As Robert Langbaum suggests, the development of the dramatic monologue is the expression of the growing fear that reflection upon experience is secondary and problematical while the mind's activity itself is immediate and verifiable. The most important consequence of this movement is that it introduced a new criterion for judging art. The measure of a work's success was no longer, " How well does it reflect the way things really are," but rather, " How well does it record the way the mind really works."

But if the measure of the success of art is how well it records the way the mind really works, there are at least two principles about the texture of the work of art which are a necessary consequence of that postulate. The first corollary is that the structure must imitate the contour of thought, as

Read says; in practical terms, the organization will be associational rather than logical. Hume in his *An Enquiry Concerning Human Understanding* maintained that all objects of human reason or inquiry can be divided into matters of fact and the relations of ideas. Ideas are related in the mind through resemblance, contiguity, or cause and effect. The impact of Hume's ideas on the modern novel becomes apparent if we turn to the criticism of Ford Madox Ford, who agrees that life does not present sensory images to the mind in any logical order.[52] It is the mind which imposes an order on the chaos of sensations and images dinning at it. He says,

> We (Conrad and Ford) agreed that the general effect of a novel must be the general effect that life makes on mankind. A novel must therefore not be a narration, a report. Life does not say to you: In 1914 my next door neighbor, Mr. Slack, erected a greenhouse and painted it with Cox's green aluminum paint. . . . If you think about the matter you will remember, in various and unordered pictures, how one day Mr. Slack appeared in his garden and contemplated the wall of his house. You will then try to remember the year of that occurrence and you will fix it as August, 1914, because having had the foresight to bear the municipal stock of the city of Liege you were able to afford a first class season ticket for the first time in your life."[53]

Ford then gives a page or so of ideas in a non-logical sequence connected only by Hume's three modes of association as the mind struggles to recall the day when Mr. Slack painted his greenhouse. If the artist sets out to follow the flow of ideas as associated in an excited mind, he will find it necessary to violate the rules of English grammar, syntax, and logic wherever the mind would make a non-logical or ungrammatical association. He will have to use grotesque and

[52] See Todd K. Bender, "The Sad Tale of Dowell: Ford Maddox Ford's *The Good Soldier*," *Criticism*, IV (Fall, 1962), 353–68.
[53] Ford Madox Ford, *Joseph Conrad* (London: Duckworth, 1924), p. 180.

far-fetched imagery whenever it seems to be true to the associative pattern of the peculiar mind which he depicts.

If the poet who sets out to record the way the mind truly works must give up the standard logic, syntax, grammar, and decorum, what does he gain in return? The second corollary Ford calls the principle of the "unearned increment" and Read calls the "collage effect." Ford asserts that all modern art

> began with the—perhaps instinctive—discovery . . . that the juxtaposition of the composed renderings of two or more unexaggerated actions or situations may be used to establish, like the juxtaposition of vital word to vital word, a sort of frictional current of electric life that will extraordinarily galvanize the work of art in which the device is employed. . . . Let us put it more concretely by citing the algebraic truth that $(a + b)^2$ equals not merely $a^2 + b^2$, but a^2 plus an apparently unearned increment called $2ab$ plus the expected b^2. . . . The point cannot be sufficiently labored, since the whole fabric of modern art depends on it.[54]

A few lines of Ford's poetry will illustrate this unearned increment.

> The seven white peacocks against the castle wall
> In the high trees and the dusk are like tapestry,
> The sky being orange, the high wall a purple barrier
> The canal, dead silver in the dusk
> And you are far away.
> Yet I can see infinite miles of mountains.
> Little lights shining in rows in the dark of them;
> Infinite miles of marshes.
> Thin wisps of mist, shimmering like blue webs
> Over the dusk of them, great curves and horns of sea
> And dusk and dusk and the little village
> and you, sitting in the firelight.
>
> Around me are the two hundred and forty men of B company
> Mud-colored.

[54] Ford Madox Ford, *The March of Literature From Confucius to Modern Times* (London: Allen and Unwin, 1938), p. 734.

Going about their avocations,
Resting between their practice of the art
Of killing men,
As I too rest between my practice
Of the art of killing men.
Their pipes glow above the mud and their mud color,
moving like fireflies beneath the trees . . .[55]

Ford builds up a composed rendering of the scene at dusk in the first twelve lines quoted which has an emotional tone of calm nostalgia. The next nine lines is a composed rendering of the soldiers which has a certain emotional effect of its own. But when these two renderings are placed side by side they intensify each other. The nostalgia of the first lines becomes much more poignant through its juxtaposition with the later lines. This increased poignancy, the sharpened emotional statement, is the unearned increment. The two impressions taken together have more emotional intensity than they have separately.

Read, in *A Concise History of Modern Painting*, expresses the identical idea in his discussion of the collage: " Although the composition is derived from reality, there is no immediate perceptual image to be represented—rather a group of visual elements associated with a memory-image. These associated elements may indeed, as Picasso always insisted, be derived from visual experience; but the important distinction is that the painting becomes a free association of images (a construct of the visual imagination) and not the representation of a subject." [56] Read tells us that this was the " moment of liberation " of Western art. " The vital difference consists in whether the artist in order to agitate the human sensibility proceeds from perception to representation; or whether he

---

[55] Ford Madox Ford, *On Heaven and Other Poems* (New York: Lane, 1918), p. 29.
[56] Herbert Read, *A Concise History of Modern Painting* (New York: Frederick A. Praeger, 1959), p. 96.

proceeds from perception to imagination, breaking down the perceptual images in order to re-combine them in a non-representational (rational or conceptual) structure. This conceptual structure must still appeal to human sensibility, but the assumption is that it does this more directly, more intensely, and more profoundly in this new way than if burdened with an irrelevant representational function." [57] Thus the artist abandons representation (if he is a painter) or logical structure (if he is a writer) so as to gain the added emotional punch of the juxtaposition of logically unconnected items in imitation of a mind in a state of excitement. He thus acquires the unearned increment or collage effect.

[57] *Ibid.*

III

The Non-logical Structure of "The Wreck of the Deutschland": Hopkins and Pindar

" The Wreck of the Deutschland " is Hopkins' first mature verse, his longest poem, and by far his most puzzling work. He seems to have constructed the poem carefully, but the reason for his structure, his principle of organization, is not apparent. How did he put the poem together? What was he trying to do? He considered the poem an ode and an examination of his understanding of the Greek odes may therefore illuminate his method of composition and, at the same time, show whether or not the study of Greek lyrics could encourage the use of non-logical structure in the way Ford Madox Ford and Herbert Read demanded as a technique of modern art.

Hopkins believed that his most important literary work was to be a commentary on Greek lyric art, in comparison with which he thought his English verse unimportant. If indeed this work was ever completed, it is now lost; but the general drift of it can be reconstructed from his extant papers. It was to be in two volumes: one treating Dorian metrics, the other dealing with the technique of composition of the Greek choral and lyric odes. Subsequent scholarship tends to show that his volume on metrics was based on a misconception about

Greek verse; but his volume on structural principles has since
been at least partially verified and, in fact, shown to be a
brilliant insight into the method of composition of certain
Greek lyrics. It is unfortunate therefore that what little attention has been given to his analysis of Greek lyric art has been
concentrated on the metrical side of his study. An examination of Hopkins' theory of the structural principle of lyric
and choral odes shows: (1) that he accurately foresees Gilbert
Norwood's hypothesis about Pindar's method of composition,
(2) that Norwood's hypothesis, in turn, explains the structure
of " The Wreck of the Deutschland," and (3) that Hopkins'
theory about the organization of Greek lyrics is consistent
with Ford's theory of the unearned increment or Read's
theory of the collage effect in modern art.

Since Hopkins considered his book on Greek lyric art to
be his most important work, its loss is a great misfortune. In
a letter to Dixon on January 27, 1887, he speaks of it as
partially completed:

> I have done some part of a book on Pindar's metres and
> Greek metres in general and metre in general and almost on
> art in general and wider still, but that I shall ever get far
> on with it or, if I do, sail through all the rocks and shoals
> that lie before me I scarcely dare to hope and yet I do greatly
> desire, since the thoughts are well worth preserving: they
> are a solid foundation for criticism. What becomes of my
> verses I care little, but about things like this, what I write
> or could write on philosophical matters, I do.[1]

Four years earlier he had written to Baillie that he was about
to undertake a major work on the Greek lyric art which was
to be divided into two parts, one on meter and the other on
style. In a letter to Bridges of October 21, 1886, he outlines
the " great discovery " which presumably was to provide the
basis for his metrical study. He says, " The Dorian rhythm,

---

[1] *Correspondence*, p. 150.

the most used of the lyric rhythms, arises from the Dorian measure or bar. The Dorian bar is originally *a march step in three-time executed in four steps to the bar.* Out of this simple combination of numbers, three and four, simple to state but a good deal more complicated than any rhythm we have, arose the structure of most of Pindar's odes and most of the choral odes in drama." [2] It seems that Hopkins believed that the Greek verse, which he called logaoedic, was composed of dactylic and trochaic feet mixed indiscriminately, but that the feet were equivalent because they were isochronous. Modern classical scholarship, although not absolutely conclusive, tends to show that his theory, insofar as it describes Greek practice, is not accurate.[3] But even if Hopkins' theory of Dorian meter is inaccurate as a description of the Greek, his misconception may have influenced his English meter (or vice versa) and therefore his study would have been of great interest to the student of his poetry if the manuscript had not been lost. John Louis Bonn, S. J., whose essay, " Greco-Roman Verse Theory and Gerard Manley Hopkins," is the best study of the accuracy of Hopkins' classical metrics, says,

> In the history of the development of metrical art forms there are three things that are incontrovertible—first, that there may be a good deal of difference between the theory and the practice of a poet; second, that theories invented posteriorly to the writing of the poems by an experimentalist may have little in common with the way in which, as a creative artist, he actually conceived his rhythmic pattern; and third, that a false theory may lead to excellent metrical and architectonic effects. To these general facts the work of Gerard Manley Hopkins was no exception.[4]

It would appear therefore that the part of Hopkins' proposed book dealing with the Dorian measure is, in fact, a misconcep-

[2] *Letters*, p. 233.
[3] See John Louis Bonn, S. J., " Greco-Roman Verse Theory and Gerard Manley Hopkins," *Immortal Diamond*, pp. 73–92.
[4] *Ibid.*, p. 73.

tion which would be interesting to the modern reader because
it might illuminate Hopkins' practice, but not because it explains the Greeks' practice.

The other part of the proposed book; which was to deal
with style, has been almost totally neglected by critics and it,
unlike the section on meter, has been supported by subsequent
scholarship. In the letter to Baillie of January 14, 1883, he
explains that his book on style will be about a new structural
principle which he has discovered at work in many Greek
lyrics:

> My thought is that in any lyric passage of the tragic poets
> (perhaps not so much in Euripides as in the others) there
> are—usually; I will not say always, it is not likely—two strains
> of thought running together and like counterpointed; the
> overthought that which everybody, editors, see (when one
> does see anything—which in the great corruption of the text
> and original obscurity of the diction is not everywhere) and
> which might for instance be abridged or paraphrased in
> square marginal blocks as in some books carefully written;
> the other, the underthought, conveyed chiefly in the choice
> of metaphors etc. used and often only half realized by the
> poet himself, not necessarily having any connection with the
> subject in hand but usually having a connection and sug-
> gested by some circumstance of the scene or of the story.[5]

To illustrate the principle of underthought which governs
imagery, Hopkins offers the first chorus of Aeschylus' *Suppliants* as an example. He says, " The underthought which plays
through this is that the Danaids flying from their cousins are
like their own ancestress Io teazed by the gadfly and caressed
by Zeus and the rest of that foolery." [6] This chorus, indeed,
demonstrates puzzling diction and metaphors. For example,
lines 4 and 5: " δῖαν δὲ λιποῦσαι χθόνα σύγχορτον Συρίᾳ
φεύγομεν " (Leaving the holy land *chorton* with Syria we
flee). What can *sunchorton* mean? Apparently *sunchortos* =

[5] *Further Letters*, p. 252.
[6] *Ibid.*

sun, *chortos*, and *chortos* means either a feeding place or fodder especially for cattle, *grass* or *hay*, as opposed to food for man, *sitos*. There is a metaphor implied in the word therefore. When the Danaids are said to leave their *chortos* which is next to Syria, clearly the author implies that somehow they are like cattle. Shortly after these lines there is an explicit mention of Io and her story. The chorus tells us about their geneology and how they found a haven in the Argive land, then they say (in lines 15–18), " κέλσαι δ᾽ Ἄργους γαῖαν, ὅθεν δὴ γένος ἡμέτερον, τῆς οἰστροδόνου βοὸς ἐξ ἐπαφῆς κἀξ ἐπιπνοίας Διὸς εὐχόμενον, τετέλεσται " (Whence our race boasts to have sprung from Zeus' engendering breath and handling of the gadfly-tormented heifer). As Hopkins points out, the " engendering breath " (*epipnoia* in line 17) by which Epaphus was conceived is echoed a few lines later in lines 27–29: " δέξαισθ᾽ ἱκέτην τὸν θηλυγενῆ στόλον αἰδοίῳ πνεύματι χώρας: "*Dexasth*' is conjectural. Probable translation: (Receive the suppliant band of women with the reverent spirit of the land). *Thelugenes* means, of course, *of female sex*, but its etymology is still strongly felt, *Thelus genesthai teat-bearing, milk-producing*. *Aidoio Pneumati* clearly echoes *epipnoia* in line 17, the breath by which Epaphus was begotten. Then the chorus continues (lines 30–32), ἑσμὸν ὑβριστὴν Αἰγυπτογενῆ, πρὶν πόδα χέρσῳ τῇδ᾽ ἐν ἀσώδει θεῖναι " ([Drive out] the insolent swarm of licentious sons of Aegyptus before they set foot on this marshy land.) Why *hesmon*? *Hesmos* means a swarm of insects and again, as Hopkins points out, there is an implied metaphor comparing the band of men born of Aegyptus to the swarm of gadflies which tormented Io. In short, this chorus employs a series of puzzling words which at first sight seem to be perversely unsuited to the topic and which make sense only when given a strained metaphorical meaning. Yet these words are all related to the underlying idea of the myth of Io so that again and again there is an implied comparison of the plight of Danaids and the troubles of Io. After Hopkins has examined the diction of this chorus, he summarizes his idea of overthought and underthought: "Perhaps what I ought to say is that the underthought is commonly an echo or shadow of the overthought, something like canons and repetitions in music, treated in a different manner, but that sometimes it may be independent of it. I find this same principle of composition in St. James' and St. Peter's and St. Jude's Epistles, an undercurrent of thought governing the choice of images used." [7] That is, the use of metaphor is not intended to illuminate the argument, but to suggest a logically superfluous comparison between the subject of the poem and a related story. That is a justification for the use of metaphor of which Bridges would not approve.

The modern reader takes it for granted that the vehicle of a metaphor ought to illuminate the logical meaning by illustrating its tenor and also ennoble the sentiment by attaching new and appropriate connotations to the tenor. Thus when Wyatt says, "Whoso list to hunt, I know where is an hind . . . ," *hind* is the vehicle of a metaphor which illustrates the qualities of the girl, her wildness, shyness, and beauty, and thus illuminates Wyatt's meaning. Moreover, the reader's emotional response to the word *hind* is appropriate to the sentiment which Wyatt hopes to express about the girl. But Aeschylus, in the first chorus of the *Suppliants* quoted above, seems to use metaphor differently. Saying *sunchortos* to mean *adjacent* neither illuminates the meaning nor evokes an emotion appropriate to the subject. The word *sunchortos* in itself has no connotation appropriate to the topic under discussion; but, when a series of such words occurs so as to suggest the myth of Io, collectively they refer to a story which evokes an emotion suitable for the subject. The actual metaphor is suppressed. The item to be compared to the subject of the poem

[7] *Ibid.*, p. 253.

stands quite apart from the text, governing the diction, but nowhere expressed. We have a hint of some such technique in Donne's " The Ecstasy," for example, and the practice runs throughout Greek lyric and choral odes—especially those by Pindar.

There is an apocryphal story about Pindar's style which, I believe, originated in Perrault although it has been widely quoted.[8] An admirer of Pindar mentioned the beginning of the First Olympian Ode with approval, whereupon his wife demanded a translation. He complied: " Water is indeed very good, and gold which shines like blazing fire in the night is far better than all the riches which make men proud. But, my spirit, if you desire to sing of contests, do not look for any star brighter than the sun during the day in the empty heavens, nor let us sing any contest more illustrious than Olympia." His wife was outraged because she thought that he was inventing nonsense to make a fool of her. After puzzling over an epinikian ode for an hour or two, the average reader will feel a certain, although probably suppressed, sympathy for the poor wife. Why does Pindar go to such perverse lengths to be difficult? The reader begins to suspect that it might be better to be bored to death by a simple catalogue of victors in the games than to be worried to death by this torrent of twisted imagery and oblique allusion.

Any ode will serve as an illustration; take, for example, *Pythian I.* This poem celebrates the victory of the chariot of Hiero, the tyrant of Syracuse, in the Pythian games of 470 B.C. Hiero's son, Deinomenes, ruled the recently founded city of Etna and Hiero dedicated his victory to the honor of that city. The poem seems to have very little connection with its ostensible subject. Strophe A is an invocation to Apollo's golden lyre which governs singers and dancers. Antistrophe

---

[8] See Gilbert Highet, *The Classical Tradition* (New York: Oxford University Press, 1957), p. 271.

A concerns the eagle of war which sleeps on Zeus' scepter. Epode A asserts that the creatures whom Zeus hates are astonished to hear the voice of the muses, for example Typhon crushed under snow-capped Etna. Strophe B depicts the eruption of Etna. In antistrophe B the speaker beseeches Zeus, who dwells on Etna, to grant him grace. Epode B requests that Zeus be as gracious to the city of Etna as he is to a sailor who has a favorable wind throughout his journey. In strophe G the speaker asserts that all good comes from the gods and in praising Hiero he compares himself to a skillful javelin hurler. Antistrophe G compares Hiero to Philoctetes. Epode G asserts that the victory of Hiero should be a joy to his son and therefore proposes to sing in his son's honor. Strophe D offers to sing of the sons of Pamphylae and the Heracleidae as well. So the ode proceeds presently to recount a series of historical battles and finally concludes with the assertion that the best reward is good fortune, next is fame, but whoever wins both has the highest crown of all.

It is apparent that Pindar's metaphors and allusive digressions do not illuminate the meaning of his discourse. What does the eruption of Etna or the battle of Cumae have to do with Hiero's victory? It is clear that the structure of this poem is not logical. It does not proceed through a series of connected propositions to a logical conclusion. It appears, rather, as a series of vivid images with only the most tenuous associative links between them, as the eruption of Mount Etna in antistrophe B seems to bring the poet to a discussion of the city Etna, which Hiero founded. How are these images connected? Is there any unifying element in the poem? Why does Pindar choose these particular scenes rather than others? He is, after all, quite definite in identifying each scene precisely. Why does he choose to speak of Typhon in Epode A rather than some other enemy of Zeus? In short, Pindar seems to select his images deliberately, but his principle of selection is not apparent and, whatever the principle may be, it definitely is not to choose images so as to illuminate a deductive or inductive argument.

In 1885, Gildersleeve commented on *Pythian I*, " Pindar's poems are constellations. There are figures in the heavens, a belt, a plough, a chair, a serpent, a flight of doves, but around them clusters much else. The Phorminx is the name of the constellation called the First Pythian." The golden lyre to which the invocation of the poem is addressed, he says, is the unifying element around which the imagery clusters. From this suggestion, Gilbert Norwood in his Sather Classical Lectures on Pindar in 1945 constructed a rationale for the structure of Pindar's odes.[9] He believes that Pindar uses a unique method of composition: " Beyond question here lies the greatest difference between his work and that of all other poets—a difference of poetical method naturally corresponding to the difference of fundamental interest." [10] This poetical method is, of course, non-logical: " When he gazes upon his miscellaneous material—the circumstances of the victory, the athlete's career, family, and native town, contemporary events in general and any detail in particular which his client has requested him to include—he broods emotionally upon these until there arises in his imagination some sensible object round which these varied topics may crystallize." [11] We might say that Pindar finds a single, symbolic objective correlative for his subject. It is important to note that his subject is not necessarily the athlete himself, but more likely the emotion which accompanies the victory. Pindar then allows the objective correlative to dictate his imagery and so he is able to bring together logically unconnected metaphors: " To feel them all and portray them all in terms of this symbol, this

[9] Gilbert Norwood, *Pindar* (Berkeley: University of California Press, 1945).
[10] *Ibid.*, p. 99.   [11] *Ibid.*

familiar sight—a beacon-fire, it may be, a horse, a pebble, or a sapling—which confers upon them a unity not logical but aesthetic." [12] In short, there is a key to the imagery and diction which stands outside the poem and which is intended to provide an embodiment for the emotion which the poet is trying to evoke. The proof that such a key exists is found in the nature of the diction: "We regularly come upon at least one word in the poem which cannot be understood fully or perhaps at all without reference to the symbol, and which therefore serves as a signpost or revelation of it." [13] Disparate metaphors and inappropriate diction refer to a common concept which exists outside the text. An unstated key unifies the poem.

Although Norwood's conjectures as to the various keys to Pindar's odes are not uniformly felicitous, a number are assuredly correct and, as he says, "If an ode has been proclaimed unintelligible in its whole drift, or if striking details have been given over as inexplicable by all commentators from the Alexandrians to the present day; and if this new doctrine reveals the whole poem as a unified work of art, the seemingly irrelevant items falling into place, may we not claim to have lit upon Pindar's conception of his topic and traced with some sureness the journey of his imagination?" [14] Pindar surely did not articulate this theory of key words so precisely as Norwood and, perhaps, he did not even realize that he was using a theory at all, but in practice it seems undeniable that he did allow a key word to dictate much of his imagery. This seems to be the way he assumed poetry ought to be written.

Norwood tries to recreate Pindar's process of writing *Pythian I*, quoted above: "Bidden to celebrate the aging and crafty prince, the youthful king, the newly founded city,

[12] *Ibid.*
[13] *Ibid.*   [14] *Ibid.*, pp. 118–19.

he ponders also the achievement of Hiero and his brothers in conflict with barbarians, and the Dorian constitution just granted to Aetna, a limited monarchy, a western Sparta, with freedom for its burghers. Dominating the scene of this celebration towers the Pillar of Heaven, the great volcano which but a few years before had burst into dreadful activity." [15] He tries to find the objective correlative for the emotion which these topics evoke: " All these thoughts blossom and entwine themselves till he sees the picture, the symbol round which they may be assembled. Where another would think and speak of the underlying idea, he sees and displays the visual object which represents and unites all these events, hopes, and prayers.

" This symbol is the Lyre, that χρυσέα φόρμιγξ which his illustrious prelude directly addresses, as other preludes address gods or goddesses." [16] Pindar invokes the harp because it produces the Platonic *mousike*— the spirit of order. Zeus and Hiero are identified as champions of order; the eagle of war, the titans like Typhon, the eruption of Etna, the barbarians opposing the Greeks at Salamis, Plataea, Himera, and Cumae, are the enemies of order. In this way the disparate scenes of the ode are connected. Norwood concludes, " Two things, at least, must surely be granted; first, that Pindar did not fling out a handfull of topics pell-mell; second, that had he made his symbolism entirely clear and unmistakable, he would have half ruined his ode, since the delight of such things resides not least in the eager questing of those for whom it was composed." [17] While his theory does not solve every problem in Pindar, in his commentary he resolves an impressive number of obscurities in the odes.

Norwood's hypothesis is most valuable when it reveals the

[15] *Ibid.*, p. 101.   [17] *Ibid.*, p. 126.
[16] *Ibid.*, pp. 101-2.

meaning of an otherwise difficult passage as, for example, in his discussion of the obscure lines 29 and 30 in *Pythian XI*: "ἴσχει τε γὰρ ὄλβος οὐ μείονα φθόνον· ὁ δὲ χαμηλὰ πνέων ἄφαντον βρέμει." Norwood tentatively translates, "For prosperity bringeth jealousy in equal measure, but ... he whose breath is of the earth murmureth obscurely."[18] The main problem here lies with *bremei*. How can *bremei* mean *esti*, as it apparently must? "βρέμει, which means 'utters a hoarse indistinct noise,' must by some mysterious transvaluation here be used to mean or imply merely 'lives.' 'Is that possible?' I asked myself."[19] But the difficulty is resolved when we realize that the key to this poem is *bee*: "The word βρέμει is after all quite natural from one point of view: for, instead of using 'live' or 'exist,' we may name some characteristic and vital action of the person or creature whereof we speak. ... So in our Pindaric passage: the Greek is quite normal if we take it as alluding to the 'lowly life' of some creature that hums. The symbol, in fact, of this ode is the Bee. That prophetesses were often called 'bees' is well attested."[20] Returning to the text of the poem, then, everything falls into place. Obscure diction becomes clear as related to the key words,

    (v. 2b) ὁμοθάλαμε
    (v. 4) μελίαν
    (v. 7b) ἐπίνομον
    (v. 8) ὁμαγερέα
    (v. 23) ἔκνιξεν
    (vv. 33 ff.) πυρωθέντων τρώων ἔλυσε δόμους ἀβροτάτος
    (v. 38) ἐδυνήθην
    (v. 55b) νεμόμενος
    (v. 57) γλυκυτάτα

[18] *Ibid.*, p. 121.
[19] *Ibid.*, p. 122.

[20] *Ibid.*, p. 124.

So the theory of a key word solves the puzzle of why Pindar substituted *bremei* for *esti*.

We have seen above that Norwood's hypothesis developed out of ideas which were available in Gildersleeve's commentary and elsewhere in the 1880's. Hopkins' theory of underthought and overthought in Greek lyric poetry foresees Norwood's hypothesis, and therefore this method of analysis may help to resolve some of the difficulties in Hopkins' English verse. The composition of " The Wreck of the Deutschland " marks the beginning of his adult period of poetic creation. The poem has been variously called a great dragon folded in the gate to forbid all entrance to the other poems, the incoherent raving of a madman, and an intense and immediate expression of the poet's personality. Although these descriptions seem contradictory, they have in common the assumption that there is no premeditated principle of unity in the poem, that the diverse parts have little connection one to another. It is certainly true that the poem is neither a unified description, a coherent narration, nor an argument proceeding through a series of connected propositions to a logical conclusion. Gardner maintains that the poem falls into four parts:

Part the First (stanzas 1–10):
   Meditation on God's infinite power and masterhood, on the direct mystical 'stress' or intuitive knowledge by which man, the dependent finite creature, apprehends the majesty and terror, the beauty and love of his Maker. . . .
Part the Second:
(Stanzas 11–17): Sudden, unexpected disaster overtook the *Deutschland*, with her emigrants and exiles bound for America. . . .
   (Stanzas 17–31): Amid the tumult and horror, the voice of a nun is heard calling on Christ to ' come quickly '. (She was one of five Franciscan exiles: surely Five, the number of Christ's wounds, is the symbol of Sacrifice and the heavenly Reward.) . . .

(Stanzas 32–5): Return to the theme of Part the First: the
poet adores the majesty and inscrutable wisdom of God. . . .[21]

If we grant these divisions, the question arises, "How are
these four sections connected?" If one section were removed
from the poem, its absence would hardly be noticed. For
example, the poem even seems to become more coherent when
the first eleven stanzas are omitted. What principle, then,
did Hopkins follow in constructing this poem?

Not only is the principle of organization obscure, but the
use of metaphors and images seems peculiar. For example,
in stanza 8 the poet apparently compares the moment of
revelation of God's grace to eating a blackberry,

> . . . How a lush-kept plush-capped sloe
> Will, mouthed to flesh-burst,
> Gush!—flush the man, the being with it, sour or sweet,
> Brim, in a flash, full!—Hither then, last or first,
> To hero of Calvary, Christ's feet—

It is possible that this peculiar kind of blackberry bursts suddenly and fills the mouth with its flavor all at once and thus
the vehicle of the metaphor may illustrate the suddenness with
which the revelation comes, but Bridges would surely
call this a low figure. The emotional response evoked by
sloe is hardly appropriate for God's grace and the image therefore seems contrived to no effective purpose. In general, it
seems that Hopkins goes to great lengths throughout the poem
to introduce far-fetched metaphors which neither illuminate
his meaning nor ennoble his sentiment. It seems legitimate
to inquire what reason, if any, Hopkins may have had for
using metaphor in this way.

Finally, the diction of the poem is not clear. It begins,

> Thou mastering me
> God! giver of breath and bread;
> World's strand, sway of the sea;

[21] *Poems*, pp. 220–21.

> Lord of living and dead;
> Thou hast bound bones and veins in me, fastened me flesh,

What does the third line mean? Lines 1, 2, 4, and 5 seem clear enough: "You, God, who rule me, who give life and food, who hold the living and the dead as subjects, have created me." The punctuation seems to indicate that line 3 is intended to be grammatically parallel to lines 2 and 4. It therefore should mean, "You, God, who are 'world's strand, sway of the sea.'" But does that mean that God is the strand (or rope which holds together) of the world and also the sway (or motion) of the sea? If so, in what sense is God like a rope holding the earth together or like the motion of the sea? What meaning is the metaphor intended to illustrate? Perhaps the line means that God is the dominating power (sway) of the sea and of the shore (strand) of the earth. If so, why does the poet introduce this peculiar enumeration? Why does he forget to mention that God rules the earth itself as well as the sea and the shore? If he wants to illustrate the extent of God's power, he need not choose to name only these particular items as subject to his rule. Indeed, the poet seems needlessly to limit the scope of God's dominion.

There are at least three difficulties with the structure of the poem, therefore: (1) It falls into four sections which are apparently unconnected, or very tenuously connected, in their subject matter. (2) Within those sections the poet introduces images and metaphors which neither illuminate his meaning nor introduce a sentiment appropriate to his topic. (3) The meaning of the poet's diction is not clear. In short, the poem seems carefully contrived—indeed, overwrought—but the reason for the contrivance, the principle behind the composition, is not clear. We have seen above that Hopkins had perceived in Greek lyric poetry an underthought and an overthought and that his discovery has subsequently been supported by Norwood's commentary on Pindar. We might therefore apply Norwood's method of analysis to Hopkins' poem to see whether we can discover there a structural principle similar to that of Pindar or of the Greek choral passages which Hopkins analyzed. If the presence of the difficulties in " The Wreck of the Deutschland " can, in general, be accounted for by Norwood's hypothesis, it would tend to show that Hopkins—perhaps unconsciously—was trying to write his poem in what he understood to be the manner of a Greek lyric or choral ode.

In order to understand what the " constellation " is, around which a Pindaric ode " clusters," Norwood first reviews the material on which the poet " broods " until he finds some material object around which these varied topics may crystallize. In the case of " The Wreck of the Deutschland " the material would seem to be the drowning of the nuns, the poet's own state of faith, and the separation of the English from the Roman Catholic Church. Norwood asserts that the poet constructs one symbol, a " familiar sight," which confers " a unity not logical but aesthetic " upon such diverse elements and, once we grasp this key symbol properly, we will understand why the poet introduced apparently disparate images and obscure diction into the poem.

Is there such a suppressed key image or underthought unifying " The Wreck of the Deutschland "? The nuns were drowned in a storm at sea. The wild water, therefore, manifests the awesome power of God at once cruel and kind, destroying the life of the nuns but bringing them to Heaven. Let us propose, for purposes of argument, that this is the key image—the grace and power of God, bringing physical death but eternal life, manifest and symbolized in water. Such a key image standing outside the text of the poem should dictate the choice of words and figures so as to connect otherwise logically disparate elements, if Hopkins was imitating Greek practice as he understood it. It should therefore be possible to clarify the obscure diction and metaphors which suggest liquids in terms of the key image. For example, stanza 1, line 3: " World's strand, sway of the sea." If God's grace and power is manifest in the storm at sea, it is only natural for the poet to mention specifically that God rules the sea and the strand, where in fact the wreck occurred, while neglecting to mention God's rule over the land itself. Indeed, he specifically says in stanza 34 that England has been separated from God since its break with the Roman Catholic Church and he prays for God to " shower " his grace on the dry land once more. In terms of the proposed key image, therefore, there is good reason for Hopkins' peculiar invocation.

> I am soft sift
> In an hourglass—at the wall
> Fast, but mined with a motion, a drift,
> And it crowds and it combs to the fall;
> I steady as water in a well, to a poise, to a pane,
> But roped with, always, all the way down from the tall
> Fells or flanks of the voel, a vein
> Of the gospel proffer, a pressure, a principle, Christ's gift.
>
> (stanza 4)

Gardner comments on this passage, " The two metaphysical images (hour-glass and well) convey the idea that as the physical life disintegrates the spiritual life is built up—by faith and grace." [22] It seems clear that the image of the hour-glass is intended to illustrate that life drifts away as time passes. Hopkins knew the poetry of George Herbert well [23] and the figure of the hourglass was probably suggested by Herbert's " Church Monuments ":

> Dear flesh, while I do pray, learn here thy stem
> And true descent; that when thou shalt grow fat,
>
> And wanton in thy cravings, thou mayst know,

[22] *Ibid.*, p. 222.
[23] *Correspondence*, pp. 23–24.

> That flesh is but the glass, which holds the dust
> That measures all our time; which also shall
> Be crumbled into dust. . . .

But the figure of the *well* indicates that a *vein* (or stream) of grace (Christ's gift) is filling the speaker as his life wanes. As the sand which symbolizes physical life runs out, the stream of Christ's gift rushes in, filling the speaker " steady as water in a well." Physical dust is replaced with spiritual water.

> Not out of his bliss
> Springs the stress felt
> Nor first from heaven (and few know this)
> Swings the stroke dealt—
> Stroke and a stress that stars and storms deliver,
> That guilt is hushed by, hearts are flushed by and melt—
> But it rides time like riding a river
> (And here the faithful waver, the faithless fable and miss).
> (stanza 6)

In stanza 4, the poet compares the grace and power of God (" Of the gospel proffer, a pressure, a principle, Christ's gift ") to a stream of water (a vein) flowing from the mountains into a well. Now, in stanza 6, the poet says that the *stress* (*pressure* in stanza 4) does not *spring* out of Christ's bliss and that the stroke dealt does not come first from Heaven although few people realize this to be the case. The stars and storms (presumably nature) deliver both the stroke and the stress (death and God's grace). He says,

> Stroke and a stress that stars and storms deliver,
> That guilt is hushed by, hearts are flushed by and melt—

Both death and God's grace are manifest in nature, especially in storms, and they hush guilt, wash or fill hearts and cause them to turn to liquid. The meaning of *stress* is, of course, complicated by Hopkins' coinage of the word *instress*, but there is some evidence that Hopkins thought of instress at times as analogous to a hydraulic pressure flowing through a body and filling it with power as, for example, a hydraulic press.[24]

But, he continues, death is the natural consequence of life, "But it rides time like riding a river." That is, time carries physical destruction along with it naturally as something floats on the current of a river.

> It dates from day
> Of his going in Galilee;
> Warm-laid grave of a womb-life grey;
> Manger, maiden's knee;
> The dense and the driven Passion, and frightful sweat;
> Thence the discharge of it, there its swelling to be
> Though felt before, though in high flood yet—
> What none would have known of it, only the heart, being
> hard at bay,
>
> 8
> Is out with it! Oh,
> We lash with the best or worst
> Word last! How a lush-kept plush-capped sloe
> Will, mouthed to flesh-burst,
> Gush!—flush the man, the being with it, sour or sweet,
> Brim, in a flash, full!—Hither then, last or first,
> To hero of Calvary, Christ's feet—
> Never ask if meaning it, wanting it, warned of it—men go.

In line 7 of stanza 6, the antecedent of *it* is apparently *stress* and *stroke* meaning both Christ's grace and man's death. In line 1 of stanza 7, therefore, the antecedent of *it* likewise seems to be *stress* and *stroke*. If so, stanza 7 means that the mercy and power of Christ began when he first went to Galilee.

" Warm-laid grave of a womb-life grey " (stanza 7, line 3) is a difficult line. I suspect that Hopkins intended the alliterative pattern to indicate chiasmus here, " Grey grave of a warm-laid womb-life." Although his syntax is not clear, it

---

[24] See Todd K. Bender, "Hopkins' ' God's Grandeur,' " *Explicator*, XXI (Feb., 1963), Item 55.

seems evident that he believes that the incarnation (womb-life) contains the necessity of death (grave). Both life and death are part of the incarnation.

> The dense and the driven Passion, and frightful sweat;
> Thence the discharge of it, there its swelling to be,
> Though felt before, though in high flood yet—
> (stanza 7, lines 5–7)

Here we have a summary of Christ's life. He progressed from the manger, to His mother's knee, and thence to the Passion. But what a peculiar detail of description Hopkins chooses to epitomize the suffering. Christ's Passion was a *frightful sweat* which was *discharged*. The *sweat* apparently symbolizes *Christ's gift* (see stanza 4) which flows down from the mountain into the poet filling him with grace. Lines 6 and 7 of stanza 7 seem to say that the stream of God's grace was felt before the Passion but it was Christ's suffering, his discharged sweat, which swelled the stream into the flood of Christianity. The use of the word *sweat* to signify Christ's sacrifice perhaps was suggested by the Anglo Saxon idiom for *blood*.

> What none would have known of it, only the heart, being
> hard at bay,   (stanza 7, line 8)
> Is out with it! . . . .   (stanza 8, line 1)

Apparently this means that only Christ's heart, being tormented, is able to express God's power and mercy, to discharge the sweat, which no one would have known so well if Christ had not suffered for man.

> . . . Oh,
> We lash with the best or worst
> Word last! . . .   (stanzas 8, lines 1–3)

This is perhaps intended to mean that we struggle finally with the word of God which is *best* in that it promises eternal life and *worst* in that it ordains physical death.

Then we come to the metaphor of the blackberry, completing stanza 8. The vehicle of the metaphor is clear enough:

a sloe will burst suddenly and fill the mouth with its juice
which is at once both sour and sweet. The tenor of the metaphor seems to be the moment of conversion. A man suddenly
is aware of the divine influence, at once sour and sweet
because it promises eternal life but requires physical death.
This tenor is explicitly stated in stanza 10:

> With an anvil-ding
> And with fire in him forge thy will
> Or rather, rather then, stealing as Spring
> Through him, melt him but master him still:
> Whether at once, as once at a crash Paul,
> Or as Austin, a lingering-out sweet skill,
> Make mercy in all of us, out of us all
> Mastery, but be adored, but be adored King.

In general, this first section of the poem is obscure and my
reading is therefore only tentative. The drift of the meaning,
however, seems clear enough even though some lines defy
paraphrase.

In the stanzas quoted there are four major metaphors: (1)
the speaker compared to sand in an hourglass in stanza 4,
(2) the speaker compared to water in a well in stanza 4,
(3) the Passion of Christ compared to a flood of sweat in
stanza 7, and (4) the moment of conversion compared to
eating a blackberry in stanza 8. Although the effectiveness
of the four varies, Bridges would surely object to at least
the *sloe* and the *sweat* as inappropriate. Why did Hopkins include them? If we assume that the key concept, the
Pindaric "constellation" of this poem, is the power and
mercy of God manifest in water, these four images are, of
course, unified. In stanza 7, the poet asserts that the stream
of power and mercy of God was felt before Christ's Passion
but the discharge of his sweat swelled it and brought it to the
flood. In stanza 6, it is this flood of physical death and eternal
life which the storms deliver to flush and melt men's hearts.
In stanza 8, it gushes, flushes, and fills the convert brimful

in a flash as the juice of a bursting blackberry fills the mouth and so, in stanza 4, the dust of physical life runs out as the stream of spiritual life flows down from the mountains to fill the man like a well.

The first eleven stanzas deal with the faith of the poet, the next five describe the shipwreck, while stanzas 17 to 32 deal with the drowning of the tall nun. We see the average passengers losing their lives in the water:

> They fought with God's cold—
> And they could not and fell to the deck
> (Crushed them) or water (and drowned them) or
>   rolled
> With the sea-romp over the wreck.   (stanza 17)

The passengers find only destruction in the water, but not so the five nuns:

> . . . sisterly sealed in wild waters,
> To bathe in his fall-gold mercies, to breathe in his all-fire glances.
>   (stanza 23)

As the water overwhelms the nun, she is suddenly and intimately aware of God:

>   . . . the Master,
> *Ipse*, the only one, Christ, King, Head:
> He was to cure the extremity where he had cast her;
>   Do, deal, lord it with living and dead;
> Let him ride, her pride, in his triumph, despatch and have done
>   with his doom there.   (stanza 28)

And so the nun's death in the water is at once a manifestation of the awesome power of God in the storm and his infinite mercy which brings her to Heaven. It is a terrible baptism.

In the remaining stanzas of the poem, Hopkins contrasts the felicity of the nun to the perilous state of England where the true faith has been rejected:

> Well, she has thee for the pain, for the
>   Patience; but pity of the rest of them!
> Heart, go and bleed at a bitterer vein for the
>   Comfortless unconfessed of them—   (stanza 31)

He again invokes God who in stanza 1 was "sway of the sea ":

> I admire thee, master of the tides,
>   Of the Yore-flood, of the year's fall;
> The recurb and the recovery of the gulf's sides,
>   The girth of it and the wharf of it and the wall;
> Stanching, quenching ocean of a motionable mind;
>
>   (stanza 32)

He implores God to bring England back to the true church before it is too late:

> A released shower, let flash to the shire, not a lightning of fire
>   hard-hurled.   (stanza 34)

Finally, he asks the drowned nun to intercede for England in Heaven:

> Dame, at our door
> Drowned, and among our shoals,
> Remember us in the roads, the heaven-haven of the
>   Reward: (stanza 35)

Roads, as here, in the plural can mean only *a place for safe anchorage*, especially since it is used in conjunction with *shoal* and *haven*. Heaven is compared to a safe harbor, whereas England is in the dangerous shoals.

Going back to the text of the poem now, we should find that there are a number of cases where peculiar diction gains new significance in terms of the key image of water symbolizing God's power and mercy. Indeed, this seems to be true:

(stanza 1) strand . . . sea
(stanza 4) water, *etc.*
(stanza 6) springs . . . flushed . . . melt, *etc.*
(stanza 7) sweat . . . discharge . . . flood
(stanza 8) gush . . . flush . . . brim . . . full
(stanza 9) storm
(stanza 10) melt
(stanza 11) flood . . . storms

(stanza 12) shoal . . . drowned
(stanza 13) haven . . . sea . . . deeps, *etc.*
(stanza 14) breakers, *etc.*
(stanza 15) lives . . . washing away, *etc.*
(stanza 16) foam-fleece . . . flood . . . wave, *etc.*
(stanza 17) drowned . . . sea romp
(stanza 18) tears . . . melting . . . river
(stanza 19) seas . . . sloggering brine, *etc.*
(stanza 20) sucked
(stanza 21) showers
(stanza 23) wild waters . . . bathe
(stanza 24) christens
(stanza 27) seas
(stanza 31) tempest
(stanza 32) tides . . . Yore-flood . . . gulf, *etc.*
(stanza 33) water . . . vein . . . plunged, *etc.*
(stanza 34) shower
(stanza 35) shoals . . . roads . . . haven

Some of these examples are clearer than others, but taken together all seem to refer to the key concept which is nowhere stated.

Norwood's hypothesis seems to fit " The Wreck of the Deutschland " well. If Hopkins wrote the poem with the underthought in mind that water manifests at once God's power and mercy, the problems in the structure of the poem are resolved. (1) The four disparate sections of the poem are connected by the unstated key. The poet examines and compares four different situations in which God's power and mercy is manifest in water. First, the poet himself, converted, is filled with God's mercy like water in a well as his physical life runs out. Second, the passengers of the Deutschland who drown see only the terrible power of God in the destructive water. Third, the nun too sees the awful power, but in her extremity realizes that God is harvesting her by means of the water, that her death is taking her to God's Heaven-haven.

Finally, the English have willfully deprived themselves of the water of faith and the poet prays that God will shower His mercy on the nation before it is too late. (2) The presence of images and metaphors which appear inappropriate can be accounted for in terms of the key concept. We have seen above how the sloe, the sweat, the well, and the hourglass are dictated by the unstated key. Although in themselves they seem needlessly contrived, they are included in the poem because they refer to the key concept. (3) The repeated use of puzzling diction referring to liquids, as for example in the mode of addressing God in stanzas 1 and 32, can also be explained by reference to the symbolic key image of water. The symbolic function of water in Christian baptism, of course, supplied this key image, ready made for Hopkins' use. As in the case of Pindar's poetry, Norwood's hypothesis does not solve every difficulty in the text, but it does supply a principle of unity, or explains the poet's method of composition, where no unity is otherwise apparent.

In a similar manner in Hopkins' shorter poems, when the logical connection of the components is least apparent, some unifying key symbol usually seems to be implied, as for example in " The Windhover." Out of all that has been written about " The Windhover," at least one fact has emerged. The poem consists of three images, the hawk, the plough, and the ember, and these three images are connected in the word *buckle*. The argument of " The Windhover " has perhaps been summarized in the opening lines of " St. Alphonsus Rodriguez ":

> Honour is flashed off exploit, so we say;
> And those strokes once that gashed flesh or galled shield
> Should tongue that time now, trumpet now that field.

Like honor, something is flashed off exploit when the hawk dives, when the plough turns the soil, when dead ashes fall from the grate and burst open revealing an inner spark. As many commentators have suggested, the real subject of the poem is stated only in the dedication: that when the Jesuit novice dedicates himself to Christ, as St. Ignatius says, he buckles on the armor of the Lord and thus becomes more honorable in God's sight. So the hawk is more beautiful when it buckles or falls, so the plough is shined when it buckles to and works, so the ash at last flashes as it buckles and crumbles away to death. The unity of this poem exists in an extended pun on the word *buckle*. The use of a pun to unify apparently unconnected elements in a poem, of course, is not unknown in English. The unity of " Lycidas " resides largely in the pun of the word *pastor*, but the structure of Milton's poem too is closely related to Greek models. The Pindaric " constellation " of " The Windhover " is the *buckle* around which the imagery clusters.

Much of Hopkins' poetry is neither unified description, nor coherent narration, nor yet an argument with logically related propositions. How, then, did he go about writing such poems? We have seen that he identified a structural principle in Greek lyrics which involves an overthought and an underthought. This structural principle has since been verified, in the case of Pindar at least, by Norwood's commentary. When we apply Norwood's method of analysis to the more obscure of Hopkins' poems, it seems to clarify at least partially the connection of the parts of the structure, to provide a reason for the intrusion of otherwise inappropriate metaphors, and to explain the significance of puzzling diction. It seems therefore that Hopkins at times, perhaps unconsciously, fell into a method of composition comparable to that of Pindar. It is possible therefore that the study of Greek lyric odes may have reinforced a fundamental proclivity toward a non-logical structure in his poetry. If Hopkins approached the Greek odes with an inclination to believe that, as Ford Madox Ford says, art must not narrate but render " various and unordered pictures," he would have found there encouragement for that belief.

IV

Non-logical Syntax: Latin
and Greek Hyperbaton

All critics agree that Hopkins seems to construct his sentences
in an unusual manner. Hostile critics maintain that his oddity
was caused by his fundamental ignorance, that he would have
written in a normal style if he had known how to do so. In
opposition, another group claims that he wrote intuitively and
therefore willfully abandoned traditional patterns of speech
because they seemed to him sterile and passionless. As we
shall see, neither of these positions is satisfactory. We must
give a closer examination to three questions: Why did Hopkins feel compelled to distort normal grammar and syntax?
Is it possible that his study of the classics could have encouraged him to do so? Is there any precedent for his practice in
the literature he knew most thoroughly?

It is generally thought that the influence of the classical
languages on English verse style is epitomized in Milton's
Latinate periods. However it seems plausible that, under the
proper conditions, the study of Latin and especially Greek
could produce a radically different effect. We have seen that
the tendency to shift attention from the nominal subject of a
poem to the way the mind of the speaker works, the tendency
to mount the psychological reaction of a peculiar character
onto the spectacle of the affair, was a distinctive artistic movement in the nineteenth century. But this practice is apparent
in both the structure of sentences and the rhetorical organiza-

tion of certain Latin and Greek poems as well. It is possible, therefore, that study of the classical languages might reinforce and encourage the kind of poetry that Richards and Read commend.

A fundamental difference between English and Latin or Greek is that the order of words in an English sentence indicates their logical relationship, whereas in Latin and Greek these same relationships of words are expressed mainly by inflection rather than position. Hence we have in both Latin and Greek the intentional placing of words in an unusual order within the sentence, called by the Greek critics *hyperbaton*, or *transposition*, which makes translation for the modern reader mainly a process of sorting or rearranging the words in a logical order.

For convenience of discussion, it is possible to identify several different kinds of hyperbaton in Greek. First, there is the placement of important words early in the sentence in violation of the logical order of ideas. This, of course, occurs at the beginning of the *Iliad*:

Μῆνιν ἄειδε, θεά, πηληιάδεω ’Αχιλῆος
οὐλομένην, ἢ μυρί’ ’Αχαιοῖς ἄλγε ἔθηκεν
(The wrath, sing goddess, of the son of Peleus, of Achilles,
Destructive, which many on-the-Greeks woes brought.)

There is a good reason to separate " wrath " by a whole line from " destructive " although the two words are grammatically connected, but that reason is not to make the sentence logically more coherent. If we discount the possibility that the opening line is fragmentary, we can only conjecture that " wrath " advances to the beginning of the line so that the main topic of the poem will be expressed in its first word. The same is true of *The Aeneid*:

Arma virumque cano, Troiae qui primus ab oris
Italiam fato profugus Laviniaque venit litora.

We often see an important word cut off from its modifiers and placed near the beginning of the sentence as a kind of topic word. A clear example occurs in *The Republic* when Plato discusses some diseases which were not known in the days of Aesculapius:

τεκμαίρομαι δέ, ὅτι αὐτοῦ οἱ υἱεῖς ἐν Τροίᾳ Εὐρυπύλῳ τετρωμένῳ ἐπ' οἶνον Πράμνειον ἄλφιτα πολλὰ ἐπιπασθέντα καὶ τυρὸν ἐπιξυσθέντα, ἃ δὴ δοκεῖ φλεγματώδη εἶναι, οὐκ ἐμέμψαντο τῇ δούσῃ πιεῖν, οὐδὲ Πατρόκλῳ τῷ ἰωμένῳ ἐπετίμησαν. (405 E)

(I make the inference [that modern doctors invent needless rules] from the fact that his sons at Troy did not scold the girl who gave to wounded Eurypylus Pramnian wine to drink mixed thickly with barley and cheese, which certainly seems to be inflammatory, nor did they reproach Patroclus who was in charge.)

Here "wounded Eurypylus" is dislocated from its logical context, separated from its proper clause, and advanced into the middle of the clause preceding it. In this way the "wounded Eurypylus" and the "Pramnian wine" are brought into juxtaposition and the contrast between them, the incongruity of the drink, is emphasized. Moreover, the order of the sentence is not written in the normal pattern of grammatical subordination, but in chronological order. The events are listed in the order in which they occurred: Eurypylus was wounded, the drink was given, the nurse was not scolded. The fact that Eurypylus was wounded is what makes the example meaningful and it is therefore advanced toward the beginning of the sentence. Hyperbaton of this type is quite common. The most striking word in the sentence is separated from the words to which it is most closely connected logically and is moved forward leaving its modifiers in their normal position.

Another common form of hyperbaton occurs when interrogatives, relatives, and conjunctions are postponed. Since these words often determine the meaning of the sentence, withholding them throws the phrase into obscurity until the last minute when parts suddenly fall into place. In Plato's *Laws*, Book VII, there is an example of a postponed interrogative which is the result of the advancement of a main word in the sentence:

> . . . μανθάνειν δὲ ἐν τούτοις τοῖς χρόνοις δὴ τί ποτε δεῖ τοὺς νέους καὶ διδάσκειν αὐ τοὺς διδασκάλους, τοῦτο αὐτὸς πρῶτον μάθανε. (810 A)
> (During these times, whatever the young are to learn or the teachers to teach—this you must yourself learn first.)

The drift of this sentence is not clear until the interrogative is revealed. Necessarily, then, attention is called to the interrogative, " *What* they are to learn." The advancement of " to learn " brings the topic word to the front of the sentence and, of course, the chiastic arrangement of *manthanein . . . manthane* stresses the paradox that the teachers must be learners as well.

A remarkable example of the postponement of a relative occurs in Plato's *Laws*, Book IX. Plato discusses the penalty proper for suicide:

> τὸν δὲ δὴ πάντων οἰκειότατον καὶ λεγόμενον φίλτατον ὃς ἂν ἀποκτείνῃ, τί χρὴ πάσχειν; (873 C)
> (What must he bear who kills the man who is said to be the nearest and dearest of all?)

Here the postponement of the relative seems to withhold the meaning from the reader until the sentence is half over. In a similar manner, Thucydides often withholds a conjunction so as to suspend the meaning of his statement until the last possible minute. He compares Sparta's treatment of allies to Athens's:

> . . . κατ᾽ ὀλιγαρχίαν δὲ σφίσιν αὐτοῖς μόνον ἐπιτηδείως ὅπως πολιτεύσουσι θεραπεύοντες, (i. 19)
> (They ruled so as to maintain an oligarchy serviceable only to themselves.)

The conjunction is postponed so that the meaning of the clause comes in a flash. The arrangement of words, of course, in this sentence is unnatural; that is, it is not the customary arrangement, and therefore it seems intentional and contrived.

A third kind of hyperbaton is the deliberate separation of logically cohering words in the line. The reader often feels that this device produces a very moving account. For example, Herodotus tells of the suicide of Adrastus, who had killed his own brother:

Ἄδρηστος δὲ ὁ Γορδίεω τοῦ Μίδεω, οὗτος δὴ ὁ φονεὺς μὲν τοῦ ἑωυτοῦ ἀδελφεοῦ γενόμενος φονεὺς δὲ τοῦ καθήραντος, ἐπείτε ἡσυχίη τῶν ἀνθρώπων ἐγένετο περὶ τὸ σῆμα, συγγινωσκόμενος ἀνθρώπων εἶναι τῶν αὐτὸς ᾔδεε βαρυσυμφορώτατος, ἐπικατασφάζει τῷ τύμβῳ ἑωυτόν. (1.45.3)

(Adrastus, the son of Gordias who was the son of Midas, he who was the murderer of his own brother and the killer of the man who had purified him, when there was no bustle of men about the tomb, seeing that he was the most unfortunate of the men he had ever known, killed himsef on the grave.)

The separation of logically cohering words can be divided into several different classifications. First, there is the division of a substantive from adjectives in agreement with it, or of a substantive from a genitive construction dependent on it. For example, in Book II of Plato's *Laws*, he speaks of education:

τούτου γάρ, ὥς γ' ἐγὼ τοπάζω τὰ νῦν, ἔστιν ἐν τῷ ἐπιτηδεύματι τούτῳ καλῶς κατορθουμένῳ σωτηρία. (653A)

(Of this [right education], as I now guess, the safety resides in well-established custom.)

Here the genitive is separated from the substantive which it modifies by the whole sentence. Quite frequently the adjective or article is separated from the noun so as to include a modifying clause which, if translated into English, produces a quaint effect, as for example, in the *Phaedo*:

ἐν τῷ πρὶν καὶ γενέσθαι ἡμᾶς χρόνῳ (88A)

(In the before-we-were-born time.)

A more complex form of hyperbaton occurs when there is a double splitting so that one hyperbaton is included within another. In Plato's *Laws*, Book VI, the proper relationship of rulers and servants is discussed in this form:

οὐδ' ἐκ τῶν ἄλλων γεωργῶν τε καὶ κωμητῶν τοῖς ἐκείνων ἐπὶ τὰ ἴδια χρήσονται ὑπηρετήματα διακόνοις, ἀλλὰ μόνον ὅσα εἰς τὰ δημόσια. (763A)

([The rulers] will not employ any servants belonging to the other farmers or villagers for their private services but only for the public requirements.)

Here *tois* is split from *diakonois* so as to include *ta idia* which is in turn separated from *huperetemata*. A third form of hyperbaton involves the arrangement of a sentence so that the logical connections seem interlaced or braided together. For example in Book VI of *The Republic* Plato says:

μηδεμίαν ἀξίαν εἶναι τῶν νῦν κατάστασιν πόλεως φιλοσόφου φύσεως. (497 B)

(No present constitution of a city is worthy of a philosophic nature.)

Such word order seems almost perverse and could hardly have been written inadvertently.

In the examples quoted, the authors seem to use hyperbaton consciously as a stylistic device. The very word *hyperbaton* in Greek indicates that the practice was recognized as something out of the ordinary. It cannot be maintained that the practice was caused by the requirements of writing in verse, because I have purposely quoted examples mainly from prose. It therefore appears that it is contrived for some artistic end. Lindhamer suggests five motives for the contrivance: (1) striving for phonetic dissimilation, especially in the case of adjectives of the first and second declension; (2) striving for

rhythmic dissimilation, or the avoidance of juxtaposed oxy-
tone words; (3) avoidance of hiatus; (4) seeking for clausula;
and (5) emphasis.[1] Denniston, however, rejects number one
and two altogether and questions number four because we
have no certain knowledge of the rhythmic laws of the Greek
clausula. He agrees that upon occasion hyperbaton is apparently used to avoid hiatus, but that by far the dominant motive
for its use is to achieve emphasis. He says, " Logically connected words stand out in higher relief when spatially separated: and, looking at the clause or sentence as a whole, alter-
nating rise and fall of emphasis produce a pleasing effect. To
this motive we must add two others: a desire to bind the
clause into a compact unity, and, in the case of Plato, a love
for pattern weaving for its own sake." [2] Denniston's explanation is not really very satisfactory. It is not clear how splitting
an important noun from its adjectives binds a clause into a
" compact unity " nor does it explain Plato's peculiar practice
to say that he liked to write that way. Plato does use hyperbaton more than most other prose writers and perhaps this
gives us a key to a major motivation for the use of hyperbaton
generally. Plato writes mainly in the form of a dialogue, of
course, and when he uses hyperbaton he is representing impromptu speech, often agitated or emotional speech.

Pseudo-Longinus in *On the Sublime* gives an explicit reason
for using hyperbaton which Denniston overlooks. Immediately before Pseudo-Longinus discusses hyperbaton, he talks
about the advantages of asyndeton, saying that just as one may
deprive runners of their speed by tying them together, so
emotion may be restrained by the use of connecting particles
and similar parts of speech and thus the sentence gains freedom

---

[1] Luise Lindhamer, *Zur Wortstellung im Griechischen* (Dissertation, Leip-
zig, 1908).
[2] J. D. Denniston, *Greek Prose Style* (Oxford: Clarendon, 1952), p. 59.
I acknowledge a great debt to Denniston's analysis and I have used his
examples where I could find none clearer.

of emotion and an effect of " coming like a missible from a
catapult " through the use of asyndeton. He puts hyperbaton
in the same category as asyndeton because hyperbaton, too,
bears the " truest character of emotion in action " (χαρακτὴρ
ἐναγωνίου πάθους ἀληθέστατος. [192v]). The question is, of
course, what does Pseudo-Longinus mean by the verisimilitude (χαρακτὴρ . . . ἀληθέστατος) which he assumes is the
object of the writer. What is it that the poet must truly
record? Pseudo-Longinus is quite explicit in On the Sublime:

ὡς γὰρ οἱ τῷ ὄντι ὀργιζόμενοι ἢ φοβούμενοι ἢ ἀγανακτοῦντες ἢ ὑπὸ
ζηλοτυπίας ἢ ὑπὸ ἄλλου τινός (πολλὰ γὰρ καὶ ἀναρίθμητα πάθη
καὶ οὐδ' ἂν εἰπεῖν τις ὁπόσα δύναιτο) ἑκάστοτε παραπίπτοντες ἄλλα
προθέμενοι πολλάκις ἐπ' ἄλλα μεταπηδῶσι, μέσα τινὰ παρεμβαλόντες
ἀλόγως, εἶτ' αὖθις ἐπὶ τὰ πρῶτα ἀνακυκλοῦντες καὶ πάντη πρὸς τῆς
ἀγωνίας, ὡς ὑπ' ἀστάτου πνεύματος, τῇδε κἀκεῖσε ἀγχιστρόφως ἀντι-
σπώμενοι τὰς λέξεις τὰς νοήσεις τὴν ἐκ τοῦ κατὰ φύσιν εἱρμοῦ παντοίως
πρὸς μυρίας τροπὰς ἐναλλάττουσι τάξιν, οὕτω παρὰ τοῖς ἀρίστοις συγ-
γραφεῦσι διὰ τῶν ὑπερβατῶν ἡ μίμησις ἐπὶ τὰ τῆς φύσεως ἔργα φέρεται.
(192 V)

(Just as when men are angry or frightened or displeased
or are carried away by jealousy or some other passion [for
there are countless emotions, more than one can mention]
then putting forward one idea; many times they leap aside
turning away from the point, inserting some illogical middle
term, and then circle back to the first idea in every way
driven before the anguish just as ships are driven before an
uncertain wind, suddenly changing the direction of the
words and ideas and changing the natural order of sequence
into countless variations, thus by means of hyperbaton an
imitation of the workings of nature is made by the best
prose writers.)

The point of this quotation is that Pseudo-Longinus is using
the phrase *mimesis . . . phuseos* (an imitation of the workings
of nature) precisely as Herbert Read demands when he says
that a poet must create " an objective equivalence of his
emotional experience: the words may not make sense, but

they make emotion—follow the contour of the thought." [3]
Pseudo-Longinus demands that a sentence, if it is to be elevated, must be constructed according to *phusis* rather than
nomos, and *phusis* apparently means the immediate, natural
flow of ideas as opposed to the final, logical disposition of
those thoughts according to the *nomos*. This idea brings to
mind, of course, Ford Madox Ford's statement that he and
Conrad decided a literary work must not be a narration or
a report, but must make the same kind of impression on the
reader that life naturally makes. That seems to be what
Pseudo-Longinus means by *ta tes phuseos erga*, the workings
of nature; the principle of verisimilitude he recommends seems
identical to the aesthetic principles of Read and Ford.

Pseudo-Longinus then gives an example of hyperbaton in
Herodotus and rewrites the line to show that it becomes dull
when the hyperbaton is removed and the sentence is restored
to natural order. Because of his use of hyperbaton, he seems
to utter thoughts forced from him and not premeditated (ὡς
μὴ δοκεῖν ἐσκεμμένα λέγειν ἀλλ᾽ ἠναγκασμένα. [193v]). The use
of hyperbaton by Thucydides shows another motivation,
however. Pseudo-Longinus says that he tries to give the impression of improvisation by making his audience fear that
his sentence will suffer a logical collapse until at the last
moment the lost word turns up at the end of the sentence and
astounds the audience with a flash of understanding. Pseudo-
Longinus makes two assumptions in this passage: (1) he believes that ideas do not cross the mind in a logical order when
it is excited, and (2) hyperbaton is intentionally used to imitate this non-logical sequence of ideas. The word order leads
the audience through the pattern of association of a mind in a
state of excitement and hence induces excitement. The inflections indicate the logical relationships of the words; the word
order indicates the order in which the words occurred to the

[3] Read, *Collected Essays in Literary Criticism*, p. 100.

speaker. This is a possible reason for the relatively more frequent use of hyperbaton in Plato's dialogue where he tries to make the speech seem impromptu by imitating the association of ideas of his speaker. Incidentally, we should note that the rise of Pseudo-Longinus' reputation in the eighteenth century is due at least in part to his implicit reinforcement of the associative theories of art which were developing at that time, leading to Wordsworth's desire for poetry which imitates " the manner in which we associate ideas in a state of excitement." And this movement probably led to Read's " collage effect " and Ford's theory of the " unearned increment " in poetry: " the juxtaposition of vital word to vital word [establishes] a sort of frictional current of electric life that will extraordinarily galvanize the work of art in which the device is employed." [4]

Ford gives us several examples of the unearned increment in both his Latin and English poetry. At the end of his *On Heaven and Other Poems*, there are several translations of his English poems. He explains that these poems were written in a contest. His friend, H. C. James, supplied the rhyme words which Ford had to use to write the English version and then James translated the poem into Latin. Ford is notoriously untrustworthy when he writes about biographical matters so it is hard to know precisely what his share in the composition of the Latin poems was. We can be certain that he at least read them carefully and recognized the principles of construction employed in them, but it is possible that he actually took a hand in the composition as well. One product of this contest is the sonnet " Sanctuary ":

> Shadowed by your dear hair, your kind soft eyes
> Look on wine-purple seas, whitening afar
> With marble foam where the dim islands are.
> We sit forgetting. For the great pines rise

[4] Ford, *The March of Literature*, p. 734.

Above dark cypress to the dim white skies
So clear and dark and still with one great star,
And marble Dryads round a great white jar
Gleam from the grove. Glimmering the white owl flies
In the dark shades . . . .
                                  If ever life was harsh
Here we forget—if ever friends turned foes.
The sea-cliffs beetle down above the marsh,
And through sea-holly the black panther goes.
And in the shadow of that secret place;
your kind, dear eyes shine in your dear, dear face.[5]

The translation of this poem into Latin hexameters seems
much better than the English, except for the last line which
is slightly bathetic because of the repetition of *benigna . . .
benigno.*

1   Caesaries teneros suavis tibi incumbrat ocellos:
2   Nos quoque contenti laetique sedemus, obliti
3   Si quid amari animos turbarit, et aequora soli
4   Cernimus atra procul spuma canescere salis,
5   Ultima qua franguntur terrae in litora fluetus.
6   Candida marmoreae Dryades prope dolia fulgent,
7   Pergracilisque pinus miscetur imagine coeli
8   (omnes exsuperans herbas, abrasque cupressos)
9   Unica qua Veneris constanter stella refulget
10 Per tenebras radians Stygias. Umbris in opacis
11 Noctua sublustris volitat . . . .
12 Si quid acerbi inerat vitae, si fallimur usque
13 Quod nimium credimus, nobis nunc omnia cedunt.
14 Imminet et scopulas praeceps aequoribus atris;
15 Perque herbas niger insepit pantaera marinas,
16 Longae iam subeunt umbrae, sed lumina semper
17 Vestra benigna mihi fulgent ex ore benigno.

The use of well-defined forms of hyperbaton in this poem is
clear. In line 1, there is interlacing, " Caesaries teneros suavis
. . . ocellos "; likewise in lines 9 and 10, ". . . Stella . . . per
tenebras radians Stygias . . ."; or in line 4, ". . . cernimus atra

---

[5] *On Heaven and Other Poems* (London: John Lane, 1918), pp. 114–15.

procul spuma. . . ." Hyperbaton is used to include a phrase
between substantive and modifying adjective in line 6, " Candida marmoreae Dryades prope dolia . . ."; or in line 9, ". . .
Unica qua Veneris constanter stella. . . ." There is double
inclusion in line 15 with one hyperbaton inside another," . . .
herbas niger insepit pantaera marinas. . . ." Advancement of
a word occurs in lines 10 and 11, " Umbris in opacis noctua
sublustris volitat. . . ." This Latin poem, therefore, demonstrates the major recognized patterns of word order which
the Greek critics called hyperbaton. But, moreover, there is
a tendency in this poem for the unnaturally juxtaposed words
to supply a logically irrelevant point of comparison between
the two items mentioned. So in line 1, the juxtaposition of
teneros and *suavis* stresses the point that the girl's little eyes
and her hair are both agreeable. We now know that Ford
organized the sequence of ideas in his stream of consciousness
monologues in his novels according to the principles of association suggested by Hume: similarity or contrast, contiguity,
and cause or effect.[6] These principles of association seem to
dictate the word order in the more violent hyperbata in this
Latin poem as well. In line 1, *teneros* suggests *suavis* because
of their similarity. In line 10, " shadow " suggests " shining "
because it contrasts. In line 6, however, the rationale behind
the hyperbaton seems somewhat different. Ford wanted verisimilitude in art, by which he meant an imitation of the way
the mind works when it imposes order on the chaos of incoming sensations and confused memories. Line 6 of the
Latin poem is simply such a representation of the mind at
work, trying to make sense of incoming sensations which
are not altogether clear in the twilight. Suppose this sentence
were read aloud. The hearer could not know what the intended logical relationship of the words was until the sentence

---

[6] See Bender, " The Sad Tale of Dowell: Ford Madox Ford's *The Good
Soldier*."

was complete. He therefore would think, " White things. Of marble. Around vases they shine." There are, therefore, two reasons for the more violent hyperbata in these lines. (1) The order of words is sometimes intended to show the mind in the process of associating ideas according to Hume's laws of association. (2) The order of words is intended to record truly the chaos of incoming sensations and random memories upon which the mind imposes a logical order. The word order becomes a tool for mounting for psychological reaction of one of the characters onto the spectacle of the affair.

In the same way, Walter Savage Landor tries to represent the flow of a character's thoughts in his monologues. Broken or fragmentary diction indicates a state of agitation in the character speaking. In " The Last of Ulysses," for example, Penelope has been granted extended beauty while waiting for the return of Ulysses but Venus, in jealousy, hopes to make her marry one of the suitors. Venus approaches the sleeping Penelope and, seeing her for the first time, speaks a soliloquy:

> " If Paris had beheld thee . . but just then
> Thy husband took thee from the Spartan land . .
> I was wrong then . . I am much wiser now . .
> But, had he seen thee, he, his house, his realm,
> Had still been safe; no guest betraid, no wrath,
> By armure ript from heroes drag'd thro' dust,
> By temples sunk in ashes, by the wounds
> Of Gods, and even their bloodshed, unappeas'd,"
> Gazing once more ere vanishing, she said
> " How beautiful! how modest! " [7]

The incoherence of the diction is intended to reflect the indecision of Venus. She is astounded by the beauty of Penelope and disconnected thoughts flash across her mind. Landor

[7] T. Earle Welby (ed.), *The Works of Walter Savage Landor*, I (London: Chapman and Hall, 1927), p. 121.

tries to imitate these mental processes and as a result his logical statement disintegrates for the first four lines quoted above.

The attempt to copy the associative process of an agitated mind destroys the logic of the sentence in English. But Landor published this poem in Latin in *Idyllia Heroica*, 1820; an English text did not appear until 1847. Therefore, as in the composition of *Gebir*, Landor wrote a Latin version before the English. The speech of Venus, quoted above, is in fact a close translation from Landor's own Latin. When he first wrote this speech Venus said,

> "Si te olim Spartae . . sed eras abducta marito . .
> Viderat Idaeus . . feci inconsulta . . maneret
> Ipse, domus, regnum, neque in Ilion, hospite laeso,
> Illa ducum exuviis, cinere implacabilis urbis,
> Deletoque opere atque effuso sanguine divum,
> Ex Agamemnoniis proruperat ira Mycenis." [8]

These lines differ from the English version in several important ways. First, in the English lines there is little syntactical connection between the fragmentary phrases. This is not true in the Latin. Two clauses are inserted into an otherwise normal Latin sentence. " Si te olim Spartae . . . viderat Idaeus . . . maneret ipse, domus, regnum, neque in Ilion, hospite laeso, Illa ducum exuviis, cinere implacabilis urbis, deletoque opere atque effuso sanguine divum, ex Agamemnoniis proruperat ira Mycenis " seems to be a normal sentence which, incidentally, employs several of the common modes of hyperbaton. It says, " If Paris had once seen *you* at Sparta, he himself, his house, and his kingdom would have endured and that implacable wrath would not have burst forth [when the hospitality was abused] from Agamemnonian Mycenae into Ilium with the arms of the leaders, the destruction of the town, and the waste of effort and bloodshed of the gods."

---

[8] Walter Savage Landor, " Ulysses in Argiripa," *Poemata et Inscriptiones* (London: Edward Moxon, 1847), p. 102.

Into this sentence, Landor inserts two unconnected phrases, "Sed eras abducta marito," (but you were taken away by your husband) and, "Feci inconsulta," (I made a mistake). Although the word order is deformed in Latin just as it is in English, the Latin sentence is logically coherent while the English is not. A fundamental difference between the two languages is that the word order in Latin can be used to represent a non-logical pattern of thought while the logical statement remains unimpaired, but such word order in English leads to incoherence.

The most interesting element in this passage, however, is that Landor himself makes the pattern of association clear. Why is the phrase, "Sed Eras abducta marito," inserted in the sentence? The answer lies in the word *Spartae*. In the Latin, "Si te olim Spartae . . sed eras abducta marito . . Viderat Idaeus . ., *Spartae* is in the locative case and modifies *viderat*: "If Paris had seen you at Sparta. . . ." But Landor translates these lines, "If Paris had beheld thee . . but just then thy husband took thee from the Spartan land. . . ." In his translation, Landor transfers the word *Spartae* into the wrong clause. It would seem therefore that the word *Spartae* connects the two clauses in his mind. The occurrence of the word in the first clause would therefore suggest the second by a non-logical association of ideas. The association follows Hume's rules, of course, if we supply the missing term, "If only Paris had seen you, but [he could not because] you were led away by your husband." The study of Latin reinforced for Landor the theory that a poem should truly represent the association of ideas of a mind in a state of excitement. He learned in Latin to copy the flow of a character's ideas in the word order of a sentence while the inflections maintained the logic of the statement. In an agitated speech there is a kind of friction or opposition of the two elements of the language. But when Landor tried to use the same technique in English he had no way to keep the logic of his lines from becoming disjointed. A passage which is exciting in Latin, therefore, becomes meaningless and prolix in English because the English has to repeat the Latin sentence—once to get the effect of non-logical association, a second time to get the meaning across. And this is precisely what Landor does in his translation of the speech of Venus above.

Hopkins, in preparation for his " moderations " in Classical Greats, had to practice for years in double translation from English into specified meters in Latin and Greek. Therefore if we want to see the direction of the early development of his poetic powers, we should look first to his Latin and Greek verse of which, unfortunately, very little is published—or indeed extant. There is, however, an interesting set of translations of songs from Shakespeare which were made late in Hopkins' career. These translations, in general, differ from the original in that they tend to involve the speaker in the situation. The speaker seems more directly concerned with the topic of the poem. He is more excited; his reaction to the affair is made more obvious in the Latin and especially in the Greek than in the English. For example, Bassanio's song in *The Merchant of Venice*, III, ii:

> Tell me where is Fancy bred,
> Or in the heart or in the head?
> How begot, how nourished?
> > Reply, reply.
> It is engender'd in the eyes
> With gazing fed; and fancy dies
> In the cradle where it lies.
> > Let us all ring Fancy's knell;
> > I'll begin it,—Ding, dong, bell.

Hopkins' Latin version reads:

> Rogo vos Amor unde sit, Camenae:
> Quis illum genuit? quis educavit?
> Qua vel parte oriundus ille nostra

Sit frontis mage pectorisne alumnus
Consultae memorabitis, sorores.
Amorem teneri creant ocelli;
Pascunt qui peperere; mox eumdem
Aversi patiuntur interire.
Nam curas abiisse ita in feretrum!
Amorem tamen efferamus omnes,
Quem salvere jubemus et valere
Sic, O vos pueri atque vos puella:
Eheu, heu, Amor, ilicet, valeto.
Eheu, heu, Amor, ilicet, valeto.

And this, in turn, is rendered in Greek:

οτροφή. χο-⌉ τίς ἔρωτος, τίς ποτ' ἆρ' ἁ πατρὶς ἦν;
ρευτὴς ά⌋ τίς δέ νιν τίκτει, τίς ἔθρεψεν, ἀνδρῶν ἢ θεῶν;
πότερ' αὐτὸν καρδίας ἢ κεφαλᾶς ἐτήτυμον εἴπω
τὸν καὶ πάλαι ὡς ἐπιστρωφῶντα μᾶλλον
τόπον; οὐ γάρ, οὐκ ἔχω πᾶ τάδε θεὶς δὴ τύχοιμ' ἄν.

ἀντιστροφή. χο-⌉ τὸν ἔρωτ' ἆρ' οὐχ ἑλικοβλεφάροις
ρευτὴς β' ⌋ ως ἐν ὀφθαλμοῖσι τραφέντ' ἀκούεις ταῖδα
μέν,
συνέφαβον δ' ἱμέρου καὶ χάριτος τέως νεοθαλοῦς
τηλαυγέσιν ἐν πρόσωπον τοῖς θεάτροις
τέλος ἐκπεσόντα φροῦδον, θανάτῳ φροῦδον ἔρρειν;

ἐπῳδός. κορυφαῖος] φροῦδος ἔρως, φροῦδος ἡμῖν.
ἡμιχόριον ἀ] ἀλλ' αἴλινον αἴλινον εἴπωμεν, ἄνδρες.
ἡμιχόριον β] αἴλινον γὰρ αἴλινον εἴπωμεν.
χορός] αἰαῖ,
φροῦδος ἔρως τὸ λοιπόν, φροῦδος ἡμῖν
ἔρως.

Strophe: Where of love, wherever was the homeland? Who begot it, who nourished it, of men or gods? Say truly whether it is from the heart or head and where it used to dwell. For I do not know where these things are ordained. Antistrophe: Did you not hear as children that love is nourished in intertwined glances, and the maturity of desire and loveliness fresh-budded in the face with far-shining looks at last is struck down ruined, to limp ruined to death?

Epode: Love is ruined, ruined for us. But let us sing a dirge,
a funeral song. A dirge, a dirge let us sing.
                          Oh.
Love is left ruined. Ruined for us love.

Hopkins explicitly changes the relation of the speaker to his
subject matter when he translates Shakespeare into Greek.
Phroudos hemin eros, he says, " Love is ruined *for us*." The
speaker is personally involved in the affair. It is his love which
is ruined. This involvement of the speaker, of course, is a
convention of the Greek choral ode. We are normally at least
as interested in the reaction of the chorus to the affair going
on as in whatever information they may tell us about the
affair. This is one reason why we are fascinated, for instance,
in *Oedipus The King* by the way the chorus often misin-
terprets the events of the plot. After Teiresias has denounced
Oedipus and Oedipus has accused him of plotting with Creon,
the chorus reflects on the turn of events:

στρ. β'. δεινὰ μὲν οὖν, δεινὰ ταράσσει σοφὸς οἰωνοθέτας, οὔτε δοκοῦντ᾽
οὔτ᾽ ἀποφάσκονθ᾽. ὅ τι λέξω δ᾽ ἀπορῶ. πέτομαι δ᾽ ἐλπίσιν οὔτ᾽ ἐνθάδ᾽
ὁρῶν οὔτ᾽ ὀπίσω. τί γὰρ ἢ Λαβδακίδαις ἢ τῷ Πολύβου νεῖκος ἔκειτ᾽ οὔτε
πάροιθέν ποτ᾽ ἔγωγ᾽ οὔτε τανῦν πω ἔμαθον, πρὸς ὅτου δὴ ⟨βασανίζων⟩
βασάνῳ ἐπὶ τὰν ἐπίδαμον φάτιν εἶμ᾽ Οἰδιπόδα Λαβδακίδαις ἐπίκουρος
ἀδήλων θανάτων.

(Terribly, terribly the wise prophet causes confusion, I
neither approve nor deny; I do not know what to say. I
flutter with expectations, seeing neither the present nor the
future. I never knew of a quarrel between the house of
Labdacus and that of Polybus either formerly or now which
I could bring as a touchstone in trying the public fame of
Oedipus and seeking to avenge the house of Labdacus for
the undiscovered murder.)

The choral ode often does not advance or clarify the plot;
instead, it shows the reaction of an interested party to what
is going on—often a mistaken reaction. When Hopkins translates the song from Shakespeare into a choral ode, he alters
the attitude of the speaker so that he is personally involved

in the proposition which he discusses and, therefore, the speaker is much more excited and emotional in the Greek version. The readers' interest shifts from the topic of the speech to the speaker's reaction to what is being said. The tone of the opening line of Hopkins' translation, " τὶς ἔρωτος τίς ποτ᾽ ἄρ᾽ ἁ πατρὶς ἦν," is more like the opening line of Sophocles' strophe, " δεινὰ μὲν οὖν, δεινὰ ταράσσει σοφὸς οἰωνοθέτας," than Shakespeare's original, " Tell me where is Fancy bred." By making the speaker personally involved in the outcome of the proposition which he discusses, Hopkins adopts a convention of the choral ode so as to make the psychological reaction of the speaker a main subject of attention and the psychological reaction, the emotional disturbance of the speaker, is made apparent mainly through the agitated order of the words in the line.

In Hopkins' translation, he deforms the word order into all the common patterns of hyperbaton. To list only a few examples: the advancement of an important word in line 1, *tis erotos*; the postponement of a particle in line 5, *an*; the separation of a modifying genitive in line 2, *tis . . . andron e theon*; and especially the effect of interlacing in lines 6 and 7:

> τὸν ἔρωτ᾽ ἄρ᾽ οὐχ ἑλικόβλεφάροις
> ὡς ἐν ὀφθαλμοῖσι τραφέντ᾽ ἀκούεις παῖδα μέν.

Hopkins' practice is consistent with the advice of Pseudo-Longinus to use hyperbaton to express the true character of emotion in action. Hopkins practiced this kind of double translation throughout his school days and necessarily had to ask himself before beginning each piece, " How is the speaker dramatically involved in what he says? How does he react to what he says? Is he overjoyed, grieved, or puzzled? How can I express the psychological reaction simultaneously with the logical statement of the proposition he considers? " If Hopkins did not take this approach, he could not have written a passable imitation of the prescribed Greek form. Such presuppositions about how poetry ought to be written are perhaps more likely to be accepted implicitly and unconsciously than through deliberation about the nature of art. At any rate, it is clear that Hopkins alters Shakespeare's lyrics (1) by making the speaker more intimately concerned with what he says, (2) therefore increasing the intensity of the speaker's emotional reaction to what he says, and (3) by expressing this emotional reaction mainly through the use of hyperbaton. Thus, for example, Ariel's song from *The Tempest*, I, ii, begins, " Come unto the yellow sands / And then take hands" but Hopkins' Latin reads, " Ocius O flavas, has ocius O ad arenas, / Manusque manibus jungite." The mode of address becomes more urgent through the advancement of *ocius* and, of course, the repetition and the omission of the verb. " Full fathom five thy father lies," from *The Tempest*, I, ii, becomes " Occidit, O juvenis, pater et sub syrtibus his est." This pattern of hyperbaton is identical to one quoted by Pseudo-Longinus (*On the Sublime*, 193r) from Herodotus reporting the speech of Dionysius, the Phocaean. The quoted passage postpones the salutation to the audience so as to state the disaster which occasions the speech immediately. Pseudo-Longinus explains that " so pressing was the danger that he would not even address the audience first " and as a result " his words do not seem thought out but rather wrung from him." The advancement of *occidit* and its separation from *pater* by *O juvenis* is therefore a conventional way to indicate extreme excitement. " It is engender'd in the eyes " becomes " Amorem teneri creant ocelli," and " Let us all ring Fancy's knell; I'll begin it,—Ding, dong, bell," becomes

αἴλινον γὰρ αἴλινον εἴπωμεν.

αἰαῖ

φροῦδος ἔρως τὸ λοιπόν, φροῦδος ἡμῖν

ἔρως.

These changes indicate that the emotional reaction of the speaker is given more prominence in the translations than in the original.

The Latin poem " Inundatio Oxoniana," apparently written by Hopkins in 1865, was not discovered until 1947. Gardner includes it in his third edition of the *Poems of Gerard Manley Hopkins* with this note:

> Classicists whom I have consulted are not unanimous about this poem; but the majority feel that the style, involved and obscure, is not due to metrical difficulties: 'it seems to be deliberate, and is therefore of interest in any study of the writer's development.'

The poem, however, demonstrates the familiar patterns of hyperbaton. It begins,

> Verna diu saevas senserunt pascua nubes
> Imbribus assiduis . . .
> (For a long time the vernal pastures felt the clouds
> savage with continual storms . . .)

Verna is in an advanced position; *saevas* is separated from its substantive; and so on. As in his translations from Shakespeare, Hopkins follows Pseudo-Longinus' advice to express emotion through the use of hyperbaton. *Verna* advances to the emphatic first position and there is a non-logical association of *verna* and *saevas* according to Hume's principle of contiguity. Hopkins therefore imitates the association of ideas of a mind in a state of excitement in the word order of his line in the poem just as in his later translations.

A recurrent thread in the criticism of Hopkins has been the assumption that the ellipsis and inversion in his English verse show that he was not in control of his medium or that he was forced to use inversion to make the rhyme or meter come out right. For example, Arthur MacGillivray says, " Inversion as a poetic device to allow for end rhymes is not only old fashioned but cumbersome. ' Fair thy fling,' ' Thy

creature dear,' 'mighty a master,' 'aspens dear,' 'disappoint-
ment all I endeavour end,' 'your round me roving end and
under be my boughs' are negligible compared with

> Leaves, like the things of man, you
> With your fresh thoughts care for, can you?" [9]

But Hopkins in a letter to Bridges on August 14, 1879, specifically denies this charge: "By and by, inversions—As you say,
I do avoid them, because they weaken and because they de-
stroy the earnestness or in-earnestness of the utterance. Nevertheless in prose I use them more than other people, because
there they have great advantages of another sort. Now these
advantages they should have in verse too, but they must not
seem to be due to the verse: that is what is so enfeebling." [10]
A poet, of course, if often a poor critic of his own work and
cannot judge his own motivation in a disinterested way, but
it is only fair to try to see what he might be getting at here.
He says that he avoids inversion except when it has "great
advantages," but he does not tell us what those advantages are.
In a similar manner, when Bridges accuses him of obscurity,
he replies, "Obscurity I do and will try to avoid so far as is
consistent with excellences higher than clearness at a first
reading. . . . As for affectation I do not believe I am guilty
of it." [11] He asserts that he is obscure only when it is consistent with some higher excellence, but, again, he does not
tell us what that excellence may be. It seems that the quality
which justifies obscurity in the English verse and the advantages obtained by inversion may be identical for Hopkins.
He often admitted obscurity when it imitated the mental processes in action and he found the advantage of inversion to
be that it allowed words to be arranged in a non-logical,

[9] Arthur MacGillivray, "Hopkins and Creative Writing," *Immortal Diamond*, p. 66.
[10] *Letters*, p. 89.
[11] *Ibid.*, p. 54.

associative pattern which indicates the state of excitement of
the speaker and induces a similar state in the reader.

To achieve this effect in " The Wreck of the Deutschland,"
stanzas 27 and 28, Hopkins uses inverted and broken diction
in precisely the same way as Landor in Venus' speech. He
quotes the nun's monologue when she is at the point of death;
the fragmentary diction is intended to convey her distraction.

> . . . I gather, in measure her mind's
> Burden, in wind's burly and beat of endragonèd seas.
> But how shall I . . . make me room there:
> Reach me a . . . Fancy, come faster—
> Strike you the sight of it? look at it loom there,
> Thing that she . . . there then! the Master,
> *Ipse*, the only one, Christ, King, Head:

Both Hopkins and Landor use deformed word order to imitate
the flow of thoughts across a mind in a state of excitement in
the way which Pseudo-Longinus recommends, and Hopkins
runs into the same problem in English which bothered Landor.
He has no way to maintain his logical statement once he has
given over word order to imitation of a non-logical process.
Hopkins, like Landor, is trying rather unsuccessfully to introduce a poetic technique peculiar to highly inflected languages
into English and the result is a tendency toward incoherence.

Throughout Hopkins' English poetry, he follows tendencies
apparent in his Latin verse. First, he often goes out of his way
to involve the speaker personally and intimately in what he
discusses; for example, the young sailor drowned with the
Eurydice is especially to be mourned because he dies outside
the Roman Catholic Church:

> He was but one like thousands more,
> Day and night I deplore
> My people and born own nation,
> Fast foundering own generation.

These lines, which incidentally show a common form of
hyperbaton, explain the speaker's personal concern for the

death of one sailor. In fact, the relation of the speaker to his subject matter in Hopkins' verse is seldom detached or calm.

A second tendency in both the English and Latin verse is that the principle governing the transition from one topic to another is often associative rather than logical. For example, The Leaden Echo says that there is no way to preserve beauty so,

> Be beginning to despair, to despair,
> Despair, despair, despair, despair.

But the Golden Echo immediately interrupts,

> Spare!
> There ís one, yes I have one (Hush there!).

Clearly the similarity between the sounds of the second syllable of *despair* and of the word *spare* causes a non-logical association in the mind of The Golden Echo. Hopkins is imitating the action of a mind according to Hume's principles.

Since there is a tendency in Hopkins' English poetry to construct a narrator who is intimately concerned with his subject matter and therefore in a state of excitement, and also a tendency to imitate the non-logical association of ideas in such a mind, we might expect that the word order of his English poetry, like that of his Latin and Greek, to be often unnatural. He does, in fact, employ all the familiar patterns of hyperbaton frequently. There is advancement similar to that at the beginning of the great classical epics. " The Loss of the Eurydice " begins, " The Eurydice—it concerned thee, O Lord." Or the untitled poem number 71 begins, " My own heart let me have more pity on. . . ." Postponement of an interrogative occurs, for example, in " The Wreck of the Deutschland," stanza 18:

> Ah, touched in your bower of bone
>   Are you! turned for an exquisite smart,
> Have you! make words break from me here all alone,
> Do you!—mother of being in me, heart.

An example of postponement which withholds the meaning of the sentence occurs in "(Carrion Comfort)": "Not, I'll not, carrion comfort, Despair, not feast on thee." Here *despair* looks like a verb modified by the initial *not* until the final words in the first line reveal that *despair* is a noun. Bridges, in his preface, violently deplored this tendency to confuse the function of a single word so as to suggest two different grammatical functions for it, but it is a common technical device in the Greek choral odes. Hopkins seems to use the device deliberately as, for example, in "Inversnaid":

> In coop and in comb the fleece of his foam
> Flutes and low to the lake falls home.

Because of the inversion in the second line, it is difficult to tell which word *low* modifies.

There is also the separation of grammatically connected phrases so as to indicate a non-logical association of ideas. For example, "To what serves Mortal Beauty?" begins:

> To what serves mortal beauty'—dangerous; does set danc-
> ing blood—the O-seal-that-so' feature, flung prouder form
> Than Purcell tune lets trend to? . . .

Mortal beauty is in apposition to *O-seal-that-so feature*, but the contiguity of *beauty* and *danger*, the simultaneous occurrence of them, sets off a non-logical pattern of association which Hopkins imitates by interrupting the logic of the line.

Perhaps most distinctive is his tendency to interlace sets of logically related words. For example, in "Peace,"

> When will you ever, Peace, wild wooddove, shy wings shut,
> Your round me roaming end, and under be my boughs?

Meaning, "Peace, wild wooddove, when will you ever shut your shy wings, end your roaming round me, and be under my boughs?" The same pattern of inversion occurs in "Spring and Fall."

> Leáves, líke the things of man, you
> With your fresh thoughts care for, can you?

Meaning, " Can you, with your fresh thoughts, care for the things of man, or leaves? " In all these cases, Hopkins is using identifiable patterns of non-logical word order in his English verse just as he uses hyperbaton in his Latin and Greek.

Among the unpublished notes by Hopkins on classical texts there is abundant evidence that he understood grammatical distortion, hyperbaton, and obscurity to be an expression of the thought processes of the character speaking. Hopkins' comment on the *Choephoroi*, line 725, which occurs in the unpublished MSS C.II, dated May 23, 1862, reads:

> 725. θέτο; Paley substitutes ἔθετο, but I think that the whole speech is purposely ungrammatical etc. to suit the character of the nurse: . . . witness the monstrous anacoluthon in 745–47, the probable one in 736 et. seq., the clumsy sentence in 724–28, in 738–41, the phrase εὖτ' ἂν πύθηται and the line 743: θέτο then is probably an old-fashioned country form.

From such a comment it is clear that Hopkins was learning from his study of Latin and Greek at an early age that a distortion in language indicates the way the mind of a particular speaker works.

In Ford Madox Ford, Walter Savage Landor, and especially in Hopkins, there is a strange confluence of two different, but complementary, literary tendencies. On the one hand, there is the typical Victorian distrust of the reflective faculty which induces Victorian, and indeed modern, art and criticism to turn to the activity of the mind as the only thing in the world which can be verified. This attitude produces both the artistic form of the dramatic monologue and the postwar psychological criticism of Richards and his associates. Its distinctive expression is a kind of art which mounts the psychological reaction of the observer directly onto the spectacle of the affair. Such art strives for verisimilitude, not by reflecting the external world accurately, but by imitating the way the perceiving mind works. One of the important techniques of such art involves the use of a monologue or revery to juxtapose logically disparate ideas either so as to indicate that the mind associates ideas roughly according to Hume's principles, or so as to imitate the supposed chaos of ideas upon which the mind imposes order. This artistic method dominates Ford's *The Good Soldier* and, indeed, works like Joyce's *Ulysses* and Eliot's *The Waste Land* as well. On the other hand, Ford, Landor, and Hopkins—in varying degrees, of course—studied Latin and Greek literature. In Latin and Greek composition they had to practice certain basically non-logical patterns of hyperbaton. They could perhaps feel, as Pseudo-Longinus explicitly states, that hyperbaton is often used to imitate the non-logical sequence of ideas of a mind in a state of excitement. Pseudo-Longinus claims that hyperbaton is used to achieve the same kind of verisimilitude which Richards, Read, and Ford seek—the accurate and direct record of the pattern of ideas crossing the speaker's mind. Once again, Hopkins fortuitously synthesizes two traditions. Through his study of the classics, especially Greek poetry, he accepts assumptions and learns techniques which induce a precocious development ahead of the trend in Victorian art and which foresee the critical assumptions of the postwar critics.

V

Metaphysical Imagery and Explosive Meaning: Crashaw, Hopkins, and Martial

There is no published evidence that Hopkins ever read Crashaw or Donne, yet a sizable portion of the critical writing about Hopkins assumes the direct influence of these poets over him. Phare's *Gerard Manley Hopkins*, 1933, vigorously extends the comparison which earlier critics had only suggested: " It is not only by his ingenious exaggeratedly logical intellect that Hopkins resembles Crashaw; there is also a likeness of tone more easily caught than defined." [1] She illustrates this similarity with parallel passages and concludes that " if Hopkins is to be discussed in terms of other poets the first to be dealt with is undoubtedly Crashaw." [2] The faults of the poets, too, are said to be the same, especially " the presence of one image after another that does nothing more than startle." [3] In a similar manner, David Morris' *The Poetry of Gerard Manley Hopkins and T. S. Eliot in the Light of the Donne Tradition*, 1953, assumes a direct influence between Donne and Hopkins for which there is no adequate proof. Alan Heuser, too, in *The Shaping Vision of Gerard Manley Hopkins*, 1958, asserts that Hopkins " recalls the poetry of

[1] Phare, *Poetry*, p. 8.
[2] *Ibid.*, p. 13.
[3] *Ibid.*, p. 16.

Donne, Herbert, Crashaw, Quarles, and Benlowes." [4] The comparison has been running through critical writing for the last thirty or more years.

It is possible, and indeed likely, that critics will tend to see connections between their favorite poets where, in fact, the only real similarity is that the poets in question appeal to a common critic. But there do seem to be genuine points of resemblance between Crashaw and Hopkins—the sudden rise of the reputations of both writers in the 1920's, the luxuriant style, the dramatic tone, the delight in paradox, compression, and wit. Their common admiration of Herbert, the baroque emblem, and baroque architecture has been suggested as the source of a common style. [5] An additional, and perhaps more plausible, cause of the resemblance, however, might be that *The Spiritual Exercises* of St. Ignatius Loyola and the epigrammatic poetry of Martial and other classical authors influenced both men deeply.

If Hopkins' style really resembles Crashaw's there must be some—perhaps entirely accidental—correspondence between their notions of what poetry ought to be. It is important therefore to define the points of correspondence and to trace the critical reception of Crashaw's style rather carefully with regard to these points specifically. By doing so, we can measure how far Hopkins deviated from the critical temper of his age, to what degree his taste in poetry was eccentric. For if he wrote in a style resembling Crashaw's in some specific way, approval of such characteristics is implicit in his practice. We must therefore see to what degree Hopkins' contemporaries shared his approval. Crashaw's reputation, once in eclipse, rose slowly but steadily in the nineteenth century until his apotheosis in the criticism following the publication of Grierson's *Metaphysical Lyrics and Poems*, 1921. A study of the

---

[4] Alan Heuser, *The Shaping Vision of Gerard Manley Hopkins* (London: Oxford University Press, 1958), p. 96.
[5] *Ibid.*, pp. 96–97.

critical reception of Crashaw therefore tends to confirm the notion that there was some pervasive movement in Victorian criticism and poetry leading up to postwar critical writing and that in terms of this tendency Hopkins was precocious; his practice, which unwittingly resembles Crashaw's verse, foresees by about forty years a widespread critical taste. The study of Crashaw and Hopkins must deal with three questions: (1) In what way are the two poets' styles similar? (2) Since Hopkins probably did not know Crashaw's writing, how can we account for the similarity? (3) Why does Hopkins write in this peculiar way so early, implying an approval of a poetic method which his contemporaries did not completely share?

Crashaw published *Steps to the Temple* in 1646, three years before his death. If Cowley's excellent poem, " On the Death of Mr. Crashaw," is a fair example, the initial reception of his verse must have been quite favorable:

> Poet and Saint! to thee alone are given
> The two most sacred names on earth and heaven
> The hard and rarest union which can be
> Next that of godhead and humanitie.

Perhaps a more convincing proof of his growing reputation was the appearance in 1658 of *The Upright Man and his Happy End*, which was presently answered by a poem entitled *Upon S. C. a Presbyterian Minister, and Captain, Stealing 48 Lines from Crashaw's Poems to Patch up an Elegy*. The poet who had plagiarized Crashaw was rather sharply reproved:

> Imprudent theft, as ever was exprest,
> Not to steal jewels only, but the chest.
> Not to nib bits of gold from Crashaw's lines,
> But to swoop whole strikes together from his mynes.

William Winstanley's *The Lives of the Most Famous English Poets, Or the Honour of Parnassus*, 1687, contained a section of unqualified praise for Crashaw, which is perhaps representative of the initial critical reception.

Although Crashaw's contemporaries seemed to see nothing outlandish in his work, it was inevitable that he would offend the poetic sensibilities of the English neoclassical critics. Pope sent a copy of Crashaw's poetry to a friend on December 17, 1710, along with a critical letter. Pope found Crashaw to be a poet who just barely deserved reading.

> I take this poet to have writ like a gentleman, that is, at leisure hours, and more to keep out of idleness than to establish a reputation: so that nothing regular or just may be expected of him. All that regards design, Form, Fable, (which is the Soul of poetry) all that concerns exactness, or consent of parts, (which is the body) will probably be wanting; only pretty conceptions, fine metaphors, glitt'ring expressions, and something of a neat cast of verse, (which are properly the dress, gems, and loose ornaments of poetry) may be found in these verses.[6]

Although Crashaw has a certain wit, Pope says, he carries his figures too far. As a result, Crashaw's poetry is too luxuriant and would be improved by pruning. "The Weeper" would be better if it were shorter because it is " a mixture of tender gentile thoughts and suitable expressions, of forc'd and inextricable conceits, and of needless fillers-up . . . ; From all which it is plain, this author writ fast and set down what came uppermost."[7] As critical taste developed in the eighteenth century, Crashaw's extravagant conceits and luxuriant style began to seem offensive and this error in taste was explained as the result of his lack of deliberate discipline. His reputation as a poet therefore declined and interest in his work became largely academic.

The romantic critics, however, did not see Crashaw as a

[6] George Sherburn (ed.), *The Correspondence of Alexander Pope*, I (Oxford: Clarendon, 1956), 109.
[7] *Ibid.*

writer of "profuse strains of unpremeditated art." For example, Hazlitt seems to contradict Pope on every critical point
except the final, unfavorable evaluation. In his lectures *On
The English Comic Writers*, he says,

> [Writers such as Crashaw and Donne] not merely mistook
> learning for poetry—they thought anything was poetry that
> differed from ordinary prose and the natural impression of
> things, by being intricate, far-fetched, and improbable. Their
> style was not so properly learned as metaphysical; that is to
> say, whenever, by any violence done to their ideas, they
> could make out an abstract likeness or possible ground for
> comparison, they forced the image, whether learned or
> vulgar into the services of the muses.[8]

Hazlitt asserts that these poets brought together for purposes
of comparison ideas which had no real likeness and hence their
collision did not illuminate, but obscured, the poet's meaning.
He also tells us that the object of true poetry is to deal with
elevated *ideas*, by which he seems to mean something like
image, the true sensory record of nature. If a man looks at an
object and then closes his eyes, the picture of that object in
his memory might be called an *idea*. But Crashaw's poetry is
not true to these ideas. Hazlitt therefore maintains that Crashaw is too deliberate, whereas Pope had argued that he was
not deliberate enough. By two different, and it would appear
mutually exclusive, indictments Crashaw is arraigned for com-
mitting errors in taste and style.

Despite Hazlitt's criticism, Crashaw profited from the general revival of interest in the old poets which was a consequence of the romantic movement. Coleridge, strange as it
may seem, acknowledges that the "Hymn to St. Theresa" inspired "Christabel."[9] Richard Cattermole's anthology, *Sacred
Poetry of the Seventeenth Century*, 1835, cites the admiration

[8] P. P. Howe (ed.), *The Complete Works of William Hazlitt*, VI
(London: Dent, 1931), 49.
[9] Samuel Taylor Coleridge, *Table Talk* (London: Oxford University
Press, 1917), p. 441.

of Coleridge as sufficient reason for including the poetry of Crashaw in the anthology. In 1834 Robert Willmott's *Lives of the Sacred Poets* made the first attempt at an extended biography of Crashaw. In 1857 George Gilfillon edited the works of Crashaw, and the next year another edition by W. B. Turnbull was published. Critics of the early nineteenth century did not approve of Crashaw's Roman Catholicism, but in the last half of the century a Roman Catholic intelligentsia began to develop in England and, as a result, Crashaw began to be the subject of interest because of his religion rather than in spite of it. Edmund Gosse devotes a chapter to Crashaw in his *Seventeenth Century Studies*, 1883. With regard to Crashaw's poem, " Upon the Death of the Most Desired Mr. Herrys," Gosse says, " Genuine grief does not bewail itself with this fluency, or upon so many stops." [10] He observes that Crashaw's " The Weeper " has lines that are probably the worst in all English poetry and that the poetry in general exhibits an " incurable defect of style." [11] Although Gosse's study is hostile, it indicates another cause of rising interest in Crashaw —the professional study of literature.

In 1921 Grierson included some poetry by Crashaw in *Metaphysical Lyrics and Poems of the Seventeenth Century: Donne to Butler* and in the preface to this volume, for the first time since the seventeenth century, we see unqualified praise. Grierson says, " Crashaw's long odes give the impression at first reading of soaring rockets scattering balls of colored fire, the ' happy fireworks ' to which he compares St. Theresa's writings. His conceits are more after the confectionery manner of the Italians than the scholastic or homely manner of the followers of Donne." [12] T. S. Eliot's review of Grierson's

---

[10] Edmund Gosse, *Seventeenth Century Studies* (New York: Dodd, Mead, and Co., 1897), p. 161.

[11] *Ibid.*, p. 174.

[12] H. J. C. Grierson, *Metaphysical Lyrics and Poems of the Seventeenth Century* (Oxford: Clarendon, 1956), p. xlvi.

anthology commends Crashaw as one of the poets with " direct sensuous apprehension of thoughts, or a recreation of thought into feeling." In 1927 L. C. Martin published the definitive edition, *The Poems, English, Latin, and Greek of Richard Crashaw*. It is important to note that Eliot included his review of Martin's edition of Crashaw in the collected essays, *For Lancelot Andrewes*, 1928. He selected the essays in this collection to illustrate his peculiar point of view which was " classicist in literature, royalist in politics, and anglo-catholic in religion." [13] His evaluation of Crashaw differs markedly from that of Pope or Hazlitt. Eliot says, " Crashaw's images, even when entirely preposterous . . . give a kind of intellectual pleasure—it is deliberate conscious perversity of language, a perversity like that of the amazing and amazingly impressive interior of St. Peter's. There is brain work in it." [14] His essay shows that the critical temper—in Eliot at least— has come round again to a sympathy for Crashaw's work; but it is simply appreciation, rather than information about the poetic technique of Crashaw, that Eliot gives us.

Scholarly study of Crashaw's style did not properly begin until 1925 with the publication of a study of Marino, Donne, and Crashaw by Mario Praz. In *Seven Types of Ambiguity* Empson notes that " Crashaw's poetry often has two interpretations, religious and sexual; two situations on which he draws for imagery and detail." [15] Empson quotes Crashaw's " Hymn to the Name and Honour of the admirable Sainte Teresa ":

> She never undertook to know
> What death with love should have to doe;
> Nor has she e'er yet understood
> Why to show love, she should shed blood,

[13] T. S. Eliot, *For Lancelot Andrewes* (London: Faber and Gwyer, 1928), p. ix.
[14] *Ibid.*, p. 122.
[15] Empson, *Seven Types of Ambiguity*, p. 246.

> Yet though she cannot tell you why,
> She can Love, and she can DY.
> Scarce has she blood enough to make
> A guilty sword blush for her sake;
> Yet she has a HEART dares hope to prove
> How much less strong is DEATH than LOVE.

He explains, " The ' context ' here is that a saint is being adored for her chastity, and the metaphors about her are veiled references to copulation." [16] Because this kind of imagery is the holding together of opposites, of opposed systems of judgment, it belongs to Empson's seventh type of ambiguity and he argues that such ambiguity is artistically effective: " One must not say that Crashaw described a sensual form of mysticism, only that he was content to use sexual terms for his mystical experiences, because they were the best terms that he could find." [17] Whereas Hazlitt had objected that Crashaw " brought ideas together not the most, but the least like " [18] which obscured the meaning rather than illuminating it, Empson maintains that Crashaw links together opposed system of judgment and thus produces an ambiguity which expresses an artistically desirable state of mental poise.

Two major scholarly works on Crashaw appeared in the 1930's, Ruth Wallerstein's *Richard Crashaw: A Study in the Style and Poetic Development*, 1935, and Austin Warren's *Richard Crashaw: A Study in Baroque Sensibility*, 1938. Wallerstein says, " If we study [Crashaw's] style in detail, it is only that we may fully understand the paradox of unbridled sensuousness, and unrestrained ingenuity, together aiming at abstract spirituality, which is the essence of his poetry. And the heart of that poetry lies in his transmutation of rigid forms to life." [19] Wallerstein here articulates clearly

[16] *Ibid.*
[17] *Ibid.*, p. 249.
[18] Howe (ed.), *Works of Hazlitt*, p. 49.
[19] Ruth Wallerstein, *Richard Crashaw* (" University of Wisconsin Studies in Language and Literature "; Madison: Wisconsin University Press, 1935), p. 14.

the general problem which had puzzled Pope, Hazlitt, and Empson. In order to find out what Crashaw intended, she studies influences, both literary and non-literary, on his style: Elizabethan music, Classical and Renaissance rhetoric, Ovid and Marino. Her work does not explain the problem it exposes, however, and Austin Warren extends her method in a further attempt to explain the " paradox." He studies the Laudian movement, the Counter Reformation, Crashaw's biography, baroque art in general, and the baroque emblem in particular in an attempt to understand why Crashaw tried to express abstract spiritual ideas in sensual terms. Warren's biography of Crashaw and his study of the baroque emblem seem to be the best scholarship available on these topics. In fact, Douglas Bush has called his *Richard Crashaw* " the standard critical treatment."

Warren's explanation of the encounter of sensualism and spirituality in Crashaw's lines is not entirely satisfactory, however. He observes that, if a reader actually visualizes the metaphors in Crashaw's poetry, the images often seem dazzling or awkward. For example, stanza 4 of " The Weeper ":

> Upwards thou dost weep,
> Heaven's bosom drinks the gentle stream.
> Where th' milky rivers meet,
> Thine crawls above and is the cream.
> Heaven, of such fair floods as this,
> Heaven the Crystal Ocean is.

The modern reader visualizing Magdalene weeping upward or the Milky Way as a milky river may find these lines ludicrous. Warren explains the difficulty this way: " The style is superficially imagistic, with its spears and swords and fires and floods. But the context makes it clear that the reader is not intended to visualize these objects. They are like the ideograms of the Chinese alphabet—pictures which are shorthand for concepts." [20] Thus Warren argues that there is really no conflict between sensuality and spirituality in Crashaw's verse because Crashaw's images had lost their literal meaning, had become shorthand for concepts. However, Leo Shapiro, reviewing Warren's book in *Poetry*, November, 1940, and the anonymous reviewer in *The Times Literary Supplement*, August 10, 1940, both point out that Warren's explanation of the peculiar poetic style of Crashaw seems to contradict Warren's own analysis of baroque art. On the one hand, he contends that baroque art brought a fresh life into decorative elements which had crystallized with long use:

> In the painting of the Counter-reformation, under the close surveillance of theologians, who assigned artists their subjects, and, in considerable measure, prescribed the treatment, lie incarnate the religious life of the age, its attitudes and its themes. Everywhere in Italian churches one sees depicted the new devotions—the angels, who float rosily among the clouds of Jesuit frescoes; the Holy Family; St. Joseph; the Infant Jesus, devotion particularly dear to the cloister. *The traditional themes assume untraditional treatment.*[21]

On the other hand, Warren contends that Crashaw's metaphors were intended not to be visualized. But if Crashaw is a baroque poet, as Warren contends, he should restore dignity and beauty to words whose figurative import had been obliterated by long use. If we accept Warren's own definition of baroque art, each word in Crashaw's poetry should be a center of infinite resonance, its sound, its spelling, its root, should be as many sources of images. Therefore, although the biographical and historical study in Warren's *Richard Crashaw* is of great value, his explanation of the characteristic paradox of "unbridled sensuousness and unrestrained ingenuity together aiming at abstract spirituality" in Crashaw's

---

[20] Austin Warren, *Richard Crashaw* (Ann Arbor: University of Michigan Press, 1957), p. 158.
[21] *Ibid.*, p. 64. My italics.

verse is not internally consistent, and is therefore not adequate. Doubtless there is a similarity between Crashaw's verse and other baroque forms of art, but this does not mean that the various forms of baroque art stand in a causal relationship to the verse. It is possible that the baroque emblem, baroque architecture, and Crashaw's poetry seem similar because they are motivated by a common impulse or set of attitudes.

Both Wallerstein and Warren suggest an important influence on Crashaw which might have produced a set of attitudes that would induce him paradoxically to use " unbridled sensuousness and unrestrained ingenuity " to express " abstract spirituality." Both critics mention that *The Spiritual Exercises* of St. Ignatius Loyola was a great influence on Crashaw, but neither explores fully possible consequences of that influence. Loyola's *Spiritual Exercises* is a guide for devotion which, in its full form, directs the exercitants for approximately a month. The exercises are divided into four periods: the first is a contemplation of sin whereby the exercitant seeks contrition, the second a contemplation of the life of Christ from his birth until Palm Sunday, the third a contemplation of Christ's passion, the fourth Christ's resurrection and ascension. Two main methods of contemplation, of particular interest here, in *The Spiritual Exercises* are the " composition of place " and the " application of the five senses." In the " composition of place " the exercitant is to visualize as vividly as possible the subject of contemplation. Then he asks for what he is seeking: penance, strength of spirit, strengthened love of God, or whatever is appropriate at this stage of the exercise. Then he applies each of his five senses to the subject of his contemplation which he previously has imagined in the " composition of place." Typical directions for an exercise read:

> The first prelude, a composition, which is here to see with the eye of the imagination the length, breadth, and depth of Hell.

The second, to ask for what I want: it will be here to ask for an intimate sense of the pain that the damned suffer, so that, if through my faults I become forgetful of the love of the Eternal Lord, at least the fear of pains and penalties may be an aid to me not to give way to sin.

The first point will be to see with the eye of the imagination those great fires, and those souls as it were in bodies in fire.

The second, to hear with the ears lamentations, howlings, cries, blasphemies against Christ our Lord and against all his Saints.

The third, with the sense of smell, to smell smoke, brimstone, refuse and rottenness.

The fourth, to taste with the taste bitter things, as tears, sadness, and the worm of conscience.

The fifth, to feel with the sense of touch how those fires do touch and burn souls.[22]

The striking sermon in Joyce's *A Portrait of the Artist as a Young Man* which causes the spiritual crisis of Stephen Dedalus is an example of a Jesuit's composition of hell for this exercise. " Imagine some foul and putrid corpse that has lain rotting and decomposing in the grave, a jellylike mass of liquid corruption. Imagine such a corpse a prey to flames, devoured by the fire of burning brimstone and giving off dense choking fumes of nauseous loathsome decomposition. And then imagine this sickening stench, multiplied a millionfold and a millionfold again from the millions upon millions of fetid carcasses massed together in the reeking darkness. . . ." The priest constructs a series of comparisons intended to illustrate the sensory impact of hell as powerfully, as immediately, as possible. First an image aimed at the sense of sight, then at the sense of smell, and so on through the five senses. We might say, then, that *The Spiritual Exercises* are exercises

---

[22] St. Ignatius Loyola, *The Spiritual Exercises*, edited and translated with facing English-Spanish texts by Joseph Rickaby, S. J. (London: Burns, Oates, and Washbourne, 1923), p. 40.

in the vicarious sensual apprehension of abstract ideas. Why does the exercitant struggle for this vivid apprehension of immaterial ideas? Father Rickaby, in his edition of *The Spiritual Exercises*, supplies this illuminating note on the exercises for the third week:

> In the doings and sayings of the Word Incarnate there is a quasi-sacramental virtue: the very looking on and listening does our soul good. Of the efficacy of Ignatian contemplation Newman well writes:—"Man is *not* a reasoning animal: he is a seeing, feeling, contemplating, acting animal." . . . Christianity is a history, supernatural and almost scenic: it tells us what its author is by telling us what he has done. . . . Instances and patterns, not logical reasonings, are the living conclusions which alone have a hold over the affections, or can form character. . . . You hear Spanish boys at play crying to one another, *mira, mira* (look, look). That is what St. Ignatius says to us over these mysteries of the life of Christ: Look at the author and achiever of our faith (Heb. xii.2); *mira, mira,* look at him.[23]

Since the editor of the text of *The Spiritual Exercises* introduces Newman as a commentator on Ignatius, perhaps we may forget chronology for a moment in order to examine Newman's interpretation of Roman Catholic contemplation. Although Newman wrote two hundred years after Crashaw, when he discusses contemplation he perhaps articulates some ideas which any intelligent reader, for example Crashaw, might derive from Ignatius. In *An Essay in Aid of A Grammar of Assent* Newman says, "There can be no assent to a proposition, without some sort of apprehension of its terms; . . . there are two modes of apprehension, notional and real; . . . while assent may be given to a proposition on either apprehension of it, still its acts are elicited more heartily and forcibly, when they are made upon real apprehension which has things for its objects, than when they are made in favor of

---

[23] *Ibid.*, p. 100.

notions and with a notional apprehension." [24] This "real apprehension" of the terms of an idea, according to Newman, may occur in three separate ways: (1) We may actually undergo the experience. Thus we see a tree topple over in a storm and assent to the proposition that, in fact, a tree is falling. (2) We may remember an experience just as it happened. I may recall having seen a tree topple over and assent to the proposition that it fell. This faculty of memory works, of course, for all five senses, not for sight alone. (3) But it is possible also to construct a "real apprehension" of some proposition whose terms we have never experienced at all. To obtain this kind of assent is one of the objectives of St. Ignatius' composition of place. Newman uses the very phrase, "the faculty of composition," in describing the process by which we can most heartily and forcibly bring ourselves to assent to a proposition, for example, belief in God, whose terms are abstract. *The Spiritual Exercises* advises the exercitant to compose vicariously material terms for an immaterial idea.

This, of course, is a well-known definition in modern literary criticism. In 1936 C. S. Lewis in *The Allegory of Love* defined allegory in this way: " Allegory consists in giving an imagined body to the immaterial. . . . In the world of matter, Catholics and Protestants disagree as to the kind and degree of incarnation or embodiment which we can safely try to give to the spiritual; but in the world of imagination, where allegory exists, unlimited allegory is equally approved by both." [25] In this literary sense, *The Spiritual Exercises*, indeed, represents the method of allegory, for example, the contemplation of the powers of Christ and anti-Christ:

---

[24] John Henry Newman, *An Essay in Aid of a Grammar of Assent* (London: Burns, Oates, and Co., 1870), p. 17.

[25] C. S. Lewis, *The Allegory of Love* (New York: Oxford University Press, 1958), p. 322.

The composition, seeing the place. It will be here to see a great plain, taking in all that region of Jerusalem, where is the Captain-General-in-Chief of the good, Christ our Lord; another plain in the region of Babylonia, where is the bandit-chief of the enemies Lucifer. . . .

Ask for what I want, and it will be here to beg a knowledge of the machinations of the evil bandit-chief, and aid to be on my guard against them; and a knowledge of the true life which the Sovereign and the True Captain shows forth, and grace to imitate him.

The first point is to imagine the bandit-chief of all the enemies in that great plain of Babylonia, seated, as it were, in a sort of big chair of fire and smoke,—a horrid and terrible figure.

The second, how he calls a convocation of countless demons, and how he scatters them, these to such a city and those to another, and so all the world over, leaving out no provinces, places, states, nor any private individuals.

The third, to consider the address that he makes to them, and how he urges them to cast nets and chains, so that they should tempt men first with riches. . . . Thus the first stage is to be that of riches, the second of honours, the third of pride; and from these three stages he leads on to all other vices.

In like manner contrariwise we must exercise the imagination on the Sovereign and True Captain, who is Christ our Lord.

The first point is to consider how Christ our Lord takes his stand in a great plain of that region of Jerusalem, in a lowly place, fair and gracious.[26]

The allegorical nature of such a passage is clear. The mention by Rickaby, of the " quasi-sacramental virtue " of the composition of place now takes on a new meaning in terms of literary allegory. In the composition of place an imagined body is given to the immaterial and this activity necessarily is expressed in the form of allegory. The words allegory is frequently applied to Crashaw's verse by literary critics,

[26] Loyola, *The Spiritual Exercises*, pp. 110–11.

although the nature of the *allegory* is seldom explained.[27] Lewis maintains, in his *Allegory of Love*, that all allegory is a metaphorical representation of an internal conflict of the will.

> If the allegorists had not discovered the moral conflict, they had at least discovered in it a new importance. They were vividly aware, as the Greeks had not been, of the divided will, the *bellum intestinum*. . . .
> But to be conscious of the divided will is necessarily to turn the mind in upon itself. Whether it is the introspection which reveals the division, or whether the division . . . provokes the introspection, need not here be decided. Whatever the causal order may be, it is plain that to fight against "temptation" is also to explore the inner world; and it is scarcely less plain that to do so is to be already on the verge of allegory.[28]

The significance of Lewis' observation is that the internal conflict finds its expression in metaphor. We cannot speak of, we can hardly think of, an "inner conflict" without using a metaphor. But, as Lewis asserts, "Every metaphor is an allegory in little."[29] It is clearly true that the exercitant comes to the exercises of Loyola in order to reduce his will to complete assent to Christianity. Were there no conflict of will, Lewis' *bellum intestinum*, there would be no need for the exercises. The method for reducing the will to a forcible and hearty assent is to construct a "real apprehension" of the terms of an immaterial proposition through the "composition of place" and the "application of the five senses."

The Spiritual Exercises therefore demands a sacramental view of the world and presupposes the existence of a conflict of the will which requires a symbolic expression appealing to the "desirous heart, the intuitive sense, of man."[30] Loyola's

[27] Howe (ed.), *Complete Works of Hazlitt*, p. 49.
[28] Lewis, *The Allegory of Love*, p. 60.
[29] *Ibid.*
[30] Evelyn Underhill, *Mysticism* (London: Methuen, 1957), p. 126.

writing, of course, is not an isolated phenomenon but the outstanding example of a vast body of similar literature.[31] *The Spiritual Exercises*, therefore, represents a wide-spread temper—we might even say the temper of the Counter Reformation for which St. Ignatius Loyola's Society of Jesus was the spearhead. Biographical scholarship, culminating in Warren's *Richard Crashaw*, in general confirms Crashaw's sympathy with the intellectual temper of the Counter Reformation. Warren concludes his biography of Crashaw by observing, " A sensuous nature, coupled with an ardent devotion to unseen realities: the two became approximately fused in the spiritual atmosphere and in the aesthetic of the Counter-reformation." [32] But it was not until 1954 that Martz in *The Poetry of Meditation* really opened the question of the influence of Loyola and related writers on Crashaw. Martz establishes that the structure of certain poems by Crashaw conforms to certain well-known processes of meditation. The *Scala Meditationis* by John Wessel Gansfort in the fifteenth century, popularized by Joannes Mauburnus' *Rosetum* (1494), and used as the basis for the widely known *The Arte of Divine Meditation* (1606) by Joseph Hall, supplies the principle of organization for Crashaw's hymn, " To the Name above Every Name: The Name of Iesus." [33] Likewise when Crashaw wrote his " Sancta Maria Dolorum or the Mother of Sorrows: A Patheticall descant upon the devout Plainsong of Stabat Mater Dolorosa," Martz shows that Crashaw expanded the old plainsong attributed to Jacopini da Todi according to principles of meditative exercise.[34] Martz thus establishes that Crashaw derives the principle of organization for some of his poetry from a tradition of meditative writing.

---

[31] For example see, Louis L. Martz, *The Poetry of Meditation* (New Haven: Yale, 1954), pp. 357ff. or Underhill, *Mysticism*, pp. 475ff.
[32] Warren, *Richard Crashaw*, p. 62.
[33] Martz, *The Poetry of Meditation*, pp. 61ff., 331ff.
[34] *Ibid.*, pp. 115ff.

But the influence of meditative writing, as Martz himself suggests, goes far deeper than the organization and arrangement of the parts of Crashaw's verse.

In connection with Donne and Herbert, Martz paraphrases an argument in the *Spiritual Combat* attributed to Lorenzo Scupoli, 1598. The contemplative is told that he can conquer his sensual appetites in several different ways and that these different ways are not equally satisfactory. First by sheer will power he can avoid sensual impulses. But this victory over sensuality is only temporary because he will not be able to banish sensual stimuli entirely and sensuality perhaps will overcome him by surprise, taking advantage of him when he is not aware of his danger. Martz paraphrases the answer to this danger which the *Spiritual Combat* proposes, " To avoid this, we must ourselves release these sensual impulses ' in order to give them a greater setback.' We must deliberately bring to mind whatever moved us to a given vice. Then, ' when you recognize the same emotion rising in your lower appetite, mobilize the entire force of your will to suppress it.' " [35] We have a kind of contemplative virtuosity, then, which intentionally grapples with sensually dangerous subject matter in order to reduce it to the service of Christian contemplation. The most proficient contemplative, therefore, will purposely seek to frame his contemplation in terms which are dangerous, which might seduce minds less stern. We may thus expect a paradox in the records of the most successful contemplatives. Christian ideas will often be couched in the most sensual or worldly terms. This is not evidence that the author used terms inappropriate for a religious subject through his insincerity but that the contemplative was tough-minded enough to conquer these sensual terms and reduce them to the service of Christianity.

It is possible to demonstrate a similarity between Crashaw's

[35] *Ibid.*, p. 132.

poetry and the contemplative tradition which goes beyond the principle of organization of his poems. Ignatian contemplation combines a sacramental view of the world with a spiritual unrest which seeks resolution in the contemplation of Christian ideas. Often the contemplation takes place by means of the composition of place and the application of the five senses in order to gain a hearty and forcible assent to the propositions of Christianity. The conflict of the will which motivates the contemplation necessarily is expressed in the form of a metaphor or allegory. There are three forms of metaphor which especially symbolize spiritual restlessness: [36] (1) The longing to depart from the normal world in search of peace results in the pilgrimage symbol. (2) The feeling of imperfection, the desire for that which will make the soul complete, results in the symbol of the lover. (3) The craving for purification results in the symbol of asceticism and pain. The more adept the contemplative, the more likely that his imagery will seem to be distracting, sensual, lush, or sexual, for these are the proper obstacles which he must overcome in a successful exercise. Such terms are the very tools of the exercitant by means of which he strengthens his will. As weights are lifted to strengthen muscles, so these images are mastered so as to strengthen the will.

In addition to Crashaw's poems mentioned by Martz which owe their principle of organization to contemplative literature, he wrote a group of poems that represent a systematic application of the senses to an abstract religious idea in the manner prescribed by Loyola. Representative of this group is " The Weeper," which is an application of the senses to the theological idea of Magdalene weeping. Moreover, the poem might be considered an allegory of pilgrimage because, if indeed anything at all happens, the tears go on a pilgrimage to meet Christ:

[36] Underhill, *Mysticism*, pp. 126ff.

> Wither away so fast?
> O wither? for the sluttish Earth
> Your sweetness cannot taste
> Nor does the dust deserve your birth.
> Whither haste ye then? O say
> Why ye trip so fast away?
>
> We go not to seek
> The darlings of Aurora's bed,
> The Rose's modest cheek
> Nor the Violet's humble head.
> No such thing; we go to meet
> A worthier object, Our Lord's feet.

The immaterial idea is given body so that the sight, first, may play on it:

> Hail sister springs,
> Parents of silver-forded rills!
> Ever bubbling things!
> Thawing crystal! Snowy hills. . . .
>
> Heavens thy fair eyes be,
> Heavens of ever falling stars,
> 'Tis seed time still with thee
> And stars thou sowest whose harvest dares
> Promise the earth; to countershine
> Whatever makes Heaven's forehead fine.

Thus the idea of Magdalene weeping is expressed in terms of silver rills, crystal, snowy hills, bright stars, producing a more forcible awareness of it. Then the nature of the imagery shifts so that the sense of taste may be brought to bear on the idea. The tears, since they are compared to stars and since stars form the Milky Way, presently are represented as being the cream of the Milky Way.

> Every morning from hence,
> A brisk cherub something sips
> Whose soft influence
> Adds sweetness to his sweetest lips.
> Then to his music, and his song
> Tastes of his breakfast all day long.

> When some new bright guest
> Takes up among the stars a room,
> And heaven will make a feast,
> Angels with their bottles come;
> And draw from these full eyes of thine,
> Their Master's water, their own wine.

To smile at the brisk cherub is to confess that the reader allows himself to be distracted from the contemplative business at hand, which is to apply the sense of taste to the idea of Magdalene's tears. The subject of attention in these lines is the tear, not the cherub, and the poet gives us three opportunities to apply the sense of taste to the idea of the tear— the sweet breakfast cream, the feast, and the angelic wine. This is not to defend these lines as good poetry, but rather to observe that Pope was wrong to think that Crashaw " writ fast and set down what came uppermost." These lines are a virtuoso piece of contemplation, intentionally establishing a distraction which the contemplative properly intends to overcome. Next Crashaw exercises the sense of touch:

> The dew no more will sleep,
> Nuzzl'd in the Lily's neck.
> Much rather would it tremble here,
> And leave them both to be thy tear.

The sense of smell:

> Does thy sweet breath'd prayer
> Up in clouds of incense climb?

The sense of hearing:

> Golden though he be,
> Golden Tagus murmurs though,
> Might he flow from thee
> Content and quiet would he go.
>
> Does thy song lull the air?
> Thy tears just Cadence still keeps time.

The diction and metaphors in this poem are not intended to

proceed in a logical fashion toward a rational conclusion. Instead, the diction and metaphors are marshalled so as to play the senses over an imaginary materialization of an immaterial idea in order to produce, as Newman says, a forcible and hearty assent to the proposition. It is therefore not surprising that the metaphors are ludicrous when measured by rational or logical criteria. However, the poem does not aim for a rational proof of a proposition, but a more forcible assent to a proposition which already commands the reader's rational assent.

A glance at the critical writing about Hopkins and Crashaw shows that the main point of comparison between the two poets is their similar use of luxuriant and logically superfluous imagery. The paradoxical style in Crashaw is compared to Hopkins', which Bridges, in the preface to the notes of the first edition, calls " the naked encounter of sensualism and asceticism." Both Hopkins and Crashaw discuss theological ideas in sensual terms, but there has been no adequate reason given for the existence of this similarity. Lacking any evidence that Hopkins ever read Crashaw, the critics argue that the resemblance is caused by the poets' mutual admiration for George Herbert.[37] But since the point of similarity between Hopkins and Crashaw is their use of logically superfluous and sensuous imagery, the argument that Herbert's poetry was a common influence which induced a common style is not credible. Herbert differs markedly from both Crashaw and Hopkins in his use of imagery, although there are other points of striking similarity among the three, as this typical poem by Herbert shows:

VIRTUE

Sweet day, so cool, so calm, so bright!
The bridal of the earth and sky—
The dew shall weep thy fall tonight;
     For thou must die.

[37] Heuser, *Shaping Vision*, p. 117.

Sweet rose, whose hue angry and brave
Bids the rash gazer wipe his eye,
Thy root is ever in its grave,
    And thou must die.

Sweet spring, full of sweet days and roses,
A box where sweets compacted lie,
My music shows ye have your closes,
    And all must die.

Only a sweet and virtuous soul,
Like season'd timber, never gives;
But though the whole world turn to coal,
    Then chiefly lives.

There is no luxuriance of imagery here, no paradox of logically superfluous sensual metaphor applied to a theological idea. The images are chosen to illuminate the logical statement of the poem. It is incredible that a poet would read lines like these and learn from them to write in a style like Crashaw's. The crucial difference between the imagery in Crashaw's " The Weeper," for example, and that in the poem by Herbert quoted above is that Herbert's images are selected so as to illuminate his logical statement whereas Crashaw's are not.

The Spiritual Exercises of St. Ignatius, however, represents a common influence on Crashaw and Hopkins which could account for a similarity in their poetic styles.[88] Hopkins was a Jesuit and his whole adult life was fashioned in the discipline of *The Spiritual Exercises*.[89] We can glance over Hopkins'

---

[88] Martz in *The Poetry of Meditation* argues that Crashaw and Hopkins both belong to the meditative tradition of which Loyola is an example, but he connects Hopkins to the meditative tradition through Hopkins' terms, *instress* and *inscape* (pp. 322ff.). The chronology of Hopkins' papers does not seem to warrant Martz' interpretation of *instress* and *inscape*. The influence of Loyola on Hopkins' style of writing seems evident, however.

[89] The influence of Loyola on Hopkins is treated by Downes in his *Gerard Manley Hopkins: A Study of his Ignatian Spirit*, as well as by earlier writers. No one has fully traced the possible influence of Loyola on Hopkins' distinctive poetic diction, however.

published prose and note precisely the times when he withdrew from the world to perform the full spiritual exercises. Moreover, his daily personal devotions were an abbreviated form of the full exercises. While Hopkins was performing the exercises during his Tertianship, the long retreat of November–December, 1881, and during the following year, he began to write notes on the exercises which he intended to expand into a full scale commentary on Loyola.[40]

Father Rickaby, whose commentary on *The Spiritual Exercises* was quoted above, was a contemporary of Hopkins' and his notes on *The Spiritual Exercises* have been shown to be, in general, congruent with many of Hopkins' ideas.[41] Indeed, since they undertook an almost identical program of spiritual discipline and education with the Society of Jesus at approximately the same time, it would be quite surprising if their interpretations of the spiritual exercises were fundamentally different. Although the commentary by Hopkins focuses on problems different from those which are central in Rickaby's study, there is no basic contradiction apparent between the attitudes of the two men toward *The Spiritual Exercises*. So when Rickaby speaks of the quasi-sacramental virtue of the incarnate word, the sensual apprehension of a theological idea, we may expect Hopkins to concur. Rickaby observes that the devotional activity of *The Spiritual Exercises* demands the uses of the senses: "You hear Spanish boys at play crying to one another, *mira, mira* (look, look). That is what St. Ignatius says to us over these mysteries of the life of Christ: Look at the author and achiever of our faith (Heb. xii.2.); *mira, mira*, look at him." [42] Although Hopkins does not discuss this point in his notes on the exercises, he does explicitly affirm this attitude repeatedly in his poetry, for example in "The Starlight Night":

[40] *Sermons and Devotional Writings*, pp. 107ff.
[41] *Ibid.*
[42] Loyola, *The Spiritual Exercises*, p. 100.

> Look at the stars! look, look up at the skies!
>   O look at all the fire-folk sitting in air!
>   The bright boroughs, the circle-citadels there!
> Down in dim woods the diamond delves! the elves'-eyes!
> . . . .
> These are indeed the barn; withindoors house
> The shocks. This piece-bright paling shuts the spouse
>   Christ home, Christ and his mother and all his hallows.

Let man look at nature. Let man use his senses to apprehend the reality of God and the meaning of Christ's sacrifice. The relation of Newman's theory of assent through apprehension to Loyola's spiritual exercises becomes apparent when Newman observes that a "real apprehension" can be constructed for a proposition whose terms have never been experienced at all. Newman asserts that through a "faculty of composition" he is able to construct, for instance, a real apprehension of a banana tree although he has never seen one. His homely example is simply a statement of the objective of Loyola's exercises. *The Spiritual Exercises* employs a faculty of composition to give material terms to an immaterial idea in order to obtain a forcible and hearty assent to a proposition that cannot otherwise be experienced directly through the senses.

It was Newman who received Hopkins into the Roman Catholic Church and after his conversion Hopkins taught Latin and Greek at Newman's Oratory School at Birmingham in 1867. There Hopkins received the vocation to become a priest. Throughout his life Hopkins had a great respect and affection for him.[43] In 1883 he asked Newman for permission to edit *An Essay in Aid of a Grammar of Assent* and to write a commentary upon it, but Newman gently refused his request.[44] It is clear therefore that Hopkins read his book carefully and sympathetically and found in it a reinforcement of

[43] See correspondence printed in *Further Letters.*
[44] *Ibid.*, p. 412.

ideas he already had found in Loyola—especially the idea that to produce a hearty and forcible assent to a theological proposition the faculty of composition must construct and apply the senses to material terms for the theological idea.

We have seen that Crashaw's poem, " The Weeper," follows Loyola's method of composition and application of the five senses. Such a poetic method is necessarily short on plot or story-line. The logical argument seems disproportionately slight when compared to the luxuriance of the imagery. Hopkins' early poem " The Habit of Perfection " is clearly the application of the senses to an immaterial idea:

> Elected Silence, sing to me
> And beat upon my whorlèd ear,
> Pipe me to pastures still and be
> The music that I care to hear.
>
> Shape nothing, lips; be lovely-dumb:
> It is the shut, the curfew sent
> From there where all surrenders come
> Which only makes you eloquent.
>
> Be shellèd, eyes, with double dark
> And find the uncreated light:
> This ruck and reel which you remark
> Coils, keeps, and teases simple sight.
>
> Palate, the hutch of tasty lust,
> Desire not to be rinsed with wine:
> The can must be so sweet, the crust
> So fresh that come in fasts divine!
>
> Nostrils, your careless breath that spend
> Upon the stir and keep of pride,
> What relish shall the censers send
> Along the sanctuary side!
>
> O feel-of-primrose hands, O feet
> That want the yield of plushy sward,
> But you shall walk the golden street
> And you unhouse and house the Lord.
>
> And, Poverty, be thou the bride

> And now the marriage feast begun,
> And lily-coloured clothes provide
> Your spouse not laboured-at nor spun.

Hopkins is striving for a " real apprehension " of the heavenly reward of the cloistered life. He knows at the outset that " elected silence " is superior to life in the world, but he seeks a more forcible and hearty assent to that proposition and he therefore constructs material terms for the idea so that he can systematically apply his senses to it. First the sense of hearing plays on the idea: " Pipe me to pastures still and be / The music that I care to hear." Then the sight: " Be shellèd, eyes, with double dark / And find the uncreated light." Then taste: " Palate, the hutch of tasty lust." Then smell: Nostrils, . . . What relish shall the censers send / Along the sanctuary side." Then touch: " O feel-of-primrose hands, O feet / That want the yield of plushy sward / But you shall walk the golden street."

This poem not only shows the systematic construction of images which in turn appeal to the five senses, but also shows the characteristic thinness of plot or logical argument which is apparent in Crashaw—nothing much seems to happen in the poem. Moreover, we should note that the poem is dramatic in form. The speaker addresses in turn personified silence, lips, eyes, palate, nostrils, hands and feet, and poverty. The poem therefore is in the form of a dramatic monologue or colloquy. Likewise, we should note that the poem proceeds through a number of paradoxes. The silence sings, shut lips are eloquent, closed eyes find light, the crust of the fast tastes best, and so on. We will presently discuss the significance of the dramatic form and paradoxical figures in Hopkins.

Just as Crashaw exhibits lush imagery which seems to have no logical justification in the poem even when he is not making a systematic application of the senses, so, too, Hopkins maintains a startling luxuriance of imagery throughout his work.

A few stanzas from "The Wreck of the Deutschland" (7, 8, 9), for example:

> It dates from day
> Of his going in Galilee;
> Warm-laid grave of a womb-life grey;
> Manger, maiden's knee;
> The dense and the driven Passion, the frightful sweat;
> Thence the discharge of it, there its swelling to be,
> Though felt before, though in high flood yet—
> What none had known of it, only the heart, being
> hard at bay,
>
> Is out with it! Oh
> We lash with the best or worst
> Word last! How a lush-kept plush-capped sloe
> Will, mouthed to flesh-burst,
> Gush!—flush the man, the being with it, sour or sweet,
> Brim, in a flash, full!—Hither then, last or first,
> To hero of Calvary, Christ's feet—
> Never ask if meaning it, wanting it, warned of it—men go.
>
> Be adored among men,
> God, three-numberèd form;
> Wring thy rebel, dogged in den,
> Man's malice, with wrecking and storm.
> Beyond saying sweet, past telling of tongue,
> Thou art lightning and love, I found it, a winter
> and warm;
> Father and fondler of heart thou hast wrung:
> Hast thy dark descending and most art merciful then.

Critics, not realizing that Hopkins felt that such a treatment had a quasi-sacramental virtue, are often baffled by the presentation of God as lightning and love, winter and warm, father and fondler—all in two lines. This is the sensual apprehension of a spiritual and immaterial idea taking place; the sense of touch plays over the warm grave, the taste senses the sloe at once sour and sweet, and the presence of the spirit becomes a flash like lightning.

Critical writing about Hopkins' imagery follows a pattern

identical to that about Crashaw. There were three main
responses over the years to Crashaw's verse. Pope assumed
no poet would deliberately write like Crashaw and therefore
he concluded that he "writ fast and set down what came
uppermost." Hazlitt and Gosse explained the luxuriance of
Crashaw's style as the result of insincerity. Empson thinks
that Crashaw's metaphors, whose tenor is theological and
whose vehicle is sexual, link opposed systems of judgment
and thus produce an ambiguity which expresses an artistically
desirable state of mental poise. These are the three main
arguments running through the critical reception of Hopkins
as well. Bridges, faced with what he called the "naked encounter of sensualism and asceticism" in Hopkins' verse,
explains the use of sensual imagery to express theological
ideas as the result of either a lack of skill or a lack of sincerity
in the poet. Bridges therefore finds in the poems "affectation
in metaphor, as where the hills are ' as a stallion stalwart, very-
violet-sweet,' or of some perversion of human feeling, as, for
instance, the nostrils' relish of incense ' along the sanctuary
side,' or ' the Holy Ghost with warm breast and with ah!
bright wings.' " [45] Bridges, like Pope, assumes that no one
would intentionally write in this sensual style. His argument
that Hopkins must be either careless or insincere is repeated
by De Selincourt [46] and others in subsequent criticism. On
the other hand, Richards, Empson, and others praise Hopkins'
use of imagery as if he had deliberately set out to induce a
state of mental poise or indecision in his readers. Both sides
ignore the Ignatian rationale behind Hopkins' style. The style
can be explained as a deliberate exercise of the quasi-sacramental virtue of the sensual apprehension of a theological idea.

We have seen, above, that "The Habit of Perfection" is
a systematic application of the senses which takes the form of

---

[45] Bridges' preface to the notes of the first edition.
[46] Ernest De Selincourt, "Robert Bridges," *Oxford Lectures on Poetry*
(Oxford: Clarendon, 1934).

a monologue or colloquy. Loyola's exercises customarily fall
into three parts: composition, analysis, and colloquy. Each
exercise must end with a colloquy or conversation between
the exercitant and the Father, the Son, or the Virgin, carried
on in the way friends converse or in the way a servant
addresses his master. Martz points out, however, that the
colloquy need not be strictly limited to a conversation with
the Father, Son, or Virgin. He quotes St. Francois de Sales:
"'Amidst these affections and resolutions' which follow
from meditation 'it is good to use colloquies, or familiar talk,
as it were sometime with God our Lord, sometime with our
blessed Ladie, with the Angels, and persons represented in
the mystery which we meditate, with the Saints of heaven,
with our selves, with our owne hart, with sinners, yea with
insensible creatures.'" [47] Loyola suggests that the colloquy is
an opportunity to ask for some favor, to blame oneself for
an evil committed, to discuss one's affairs and ask advice or
help. The practice of the colloquy would surely encourage
the discussion of spiritual problems in a colloquial, or conversational, manner. Hopkins practiced the colloquy in his
daily devotions and it is therefore not surprising to find that
he falls into a conversational or dramatic tone in his poems.
For example, "Nondum," written in 1866 while he was
hesitating between the Anglican and the Catholic beliefs, is
clearly a colloquy between Hopkins and God wherein Hopkins asks for help in making his decision:

> God, though to Thee our psalm we raise
> No answering voice comes from the skies;
> To Thee the trembling sinner prays
> But no forgiving voice replies;
> Our prayer seems lost in desert ways,
> Our hymn in the vast silence dies.
> . . . .
> Speak! whisper to my watching heart

[47] Martz, *The Poetry of Meditation,* p. 37.

> One word—as when a mother speaks
> Soft, when she sees her infant start,
> Till dimpled joy steals o'er its cheeks.
> Then, to behold Thee as Thou art,
> I'll wait till morn eternal breaks.

The beginning of " The Wreck of the Deutschland " has the same dramatic quality:

> Thou mastering me
> God! giver of breath and bread;
> World's strand, sway of the sea;
> Lord of living and dead;
> Thou hast bound bones and veins in me, fastened me flesh,
> And after it almost unmade, what with dread,
> Thy doing: and dost thou touch me afresh?
> Over again I feel thy finger and find thee.

Likewise " The Starlight Night " takes the form of urgent and direct address:

> Look at the stars! look, look up at the skies!
> O look at all the fire-folk sitting in the air!

" The Loss of the Eurydice," too, has this characteristic mode of address:

> The Eurydice—it concerned thee, O Lord:
> Three hundred souls, O alas! on board,
> Some asleep unawakened, all un-
> warned, eleven fathoms fallen
> Where she foundered! . . .

This is a peculiar hortatory tone which is also characteristic of Donne and which has induced critics to try to establish his direct influence over Hopkins.[48] There is, however, no

---

[48] David Morris in *The Poetry of Gerard Manley Hopkins and T. S. Eliot in the Light of the Donne Tradition* (Bern: Francke, 1953) says, " Hopkins could not have failed to have been attracted or repelled by such a kindred spirit as Donne in many ways was. Yet Hopkins, in all his letters and notebooks, never mentions Donne's name once, although he does mention his followers, Herbert, Crashaw and Vaughan. This is an astonishing thing, but it would be entirely wrong to assume

adequate evidence to prove a direct relationship between Donne and Hopkins although their poems have an uncanny similarity at times. For example, compare Donne's sonnet,

> Thou hast made me and shall thy work decay?
> Repair me now, for now mine end doth haste . . .

and Hopkins' " Justus quidem tu es . . . ,"

> Thou art indeed just, Lord, if I contend
> With Thee; but, sir, so what I plead is just.
> Why do sinners' ways prosper? and why must
> Disappointment all I endeavour end?

The similarity in tone in these two poems does not arise from a direct influence of Donne over Hopkins, but from the fact that both poems are clearly religious colloquies. Both poems are a particular kind of dramatic monologue in which the poet dramatizes his mental distress in an imaginary conversation with God.

Hopkins' practice of the Ignatian colloquy encouraged him to experiment in the techniques of the dramatic monologue. The Jesuit tradition induced him to explore this particular

that for this reason all possibility that Hopkins was influenced by Donne must be ruled out. Some writers on Hopkins, while admitting his affinity to Donne, seem to be unwilling to admit any influence merely for this reason. They seek to trace the Metaphysical element in Hopkins entirely to Herbert and Crashaw, thus admitting only indirect influence by Donne. In fact, Hopkins is often far more like Donne than either Herbert or Crashaw in his passionate intensity and his intellectual complexity. Many have observed this close similarity: thus Bullough, speaking of Hopkins' later sonnets, says: ' It is as though Donne were born again with a softer, more tremulous nature.' The fact that Hopkins never mentions Donne need not worry us unduly, since he also fails to mention other great poets whom he must have known (for he was widely read in poetry), and he does record having constantly read the critical essays of Edmund Gosse, later Donne's great biographer. It can be assumed, then, that Hopkins knew Donne's work, as he knew that of Herbert, Vaughan, and Crashaw."

I have not been able to find any evidence to support Morris' claim that Hopkins knew Crashaw's work. Morris' argument in regard to Donne needs no comment.

contemporary literary tendency and so he grapples with some of the same problems which the most traditional Victorian poets faced. For example, since a colloquy should have its proper, or colloquial diction, Hopkins must define its essential quality. In a letter to Bridges on August 14, 1879, he says, "I cut myself off from the use or *ere, o'er, wellnigh what time, say not* (for *do not say*), because, though dignified, they neither belong to nor ever cd. arise from, or be the elevation of, ordinary modern speech. For it seems to me that the poetical language of an age shd. be the current language heightened...." [49] Hopkins, of course, quotes a commonplace idea in the nineteenth century when he demands "current language heightened" in poetry. Wordsworth's preface to the second edition of the *Lyrical Ballads* says,

> The principal object, then, proposed in these Poems was to choose incidents and situations from common life, and to relate or describe them throughout, as far as was possible, in a selection of language really used by men, and, at the same time, to throw over them a certain colouring of imagination, whereby ordinary things should be presented to the mind in an unusual aspect; and further, and above all, to make these incidents and situations interesting by tracing in them, truly though not ostentatiously, the primary laws of our nature; chiefly as far as regards the manner in which we associate ideas in a state of excitement. Humble and rustic life was generally chosen, because, in that condition, the essential passions of the heart find a better soil in which they can attain their maturity, are less under restraint, and speak a plainer and more emphatic language.

As Coleridge promptly pointed out in the *Biographia Literaria,* the theory of "current language heightened" does not seem to correspond to Wordsworth's own practice. If by "current language heightened" Hopkins means the words and idioms customarily used by the average man, his statement, too, seems

[49] *Letters,* p. 89.

absurd. What laborer ever used diction such as that in " Spelt from Sybil's Leaves," for example?

> Earnest, earthless, equal, attuneable,' vaulty, voluminous, . .
>   stupendous
> Evening strains to be tíme's vást,' womb-of-all, home-of-all,
>   hearse-of-all night.
> Her fond yellow hornlight wound to the west,' her wild
>   hollow hoarlight hung to the height.

Hopkins knew Coleridge's objection to Wordsworth's theory and saw that one revolutionary aspect of Wordsworth's lyrical ballads is the use of dramatic situations in many of the poems, the use of dialogue or monologue as a structural principle. Some of the opening lines of Wordsworth's lyrical ballads seem almost to parody the dramatic form of address in, for example, Donne's " Go and catch a falling star . . ." or of Hopkins' " I wake and feel the fell of Dark, not day. . . ." Compare the opening of " The Tables Turned ":

> Up! up! my Friend, and quit your books;
> Or surely you'll grow double.

Or the opening of " Lines Written in Early Spring ":

> I heard a thousand blended notes
> While in a grove I sate reclined.

In his preface, Wordsworth does not describe these poems in a precise manner. A modern reader, looking back at Wordsworth after reading work by Eliot, Pound, Browning, or even Tennyson, sees that Wordsworth's lines are crude versions of dramatic monologue—or sometimes dialogue. It is only in this light that Wordsworth's preface makes sense. Perhaps when Wordsworth says he writes " language really used by men . . . a plainer and more emphatic language," he is really getting at the dramatic quality of his work.

Hopkins therefore tried to reconcile the theory to his practice by interpreting " current language " in terms of the dramatic situation of the speaker, rather than in terms of the vocabulary of a certain class of men. The lines quoted above from "Spelt from Sybil's Leaves" are part of a dialogue between Hopkins and his heart—indeed a colloquy of the kind suggested by St. Francois de Sales, "with oure owne hart." It is the heart which reminds him that evening draws near, "Earnest, earthless, equal, attuneable. . . ." Presently he replies to the heart and concedes that its warning was just, "Heart, you round me right with: Our evening is over us; our night whelms, whelms, and will end us." The diction of the poem is therefore colloquial in the sense that it is a colloquy written in running (or current) dialogue. Hopkins explains his theory of poetic diction in more detail in a letter to Bridges on November 4, 1882, in which he criticizes a play by Bridges because it lacks a quality of "the first importance," which he calls *bidding*, or "the art or value of saying everything right *to* or *at* the hearer, interesting him, holding him in the attitude of correspondent or adressed or at least concerned, making it everywhere an act of intercourse—and of discarding everything that does not bid, does not tell." [50] Hopkins wants diction which holds the hearer in the attitude of a correspondent.

We see, then, that Hopkins found the commonplace notion that poetic diction should be "current language heightened" redefined by the practice of the Ignatian colloquy. The Jesuit tradition strengthened the Victorian idea and gave it a definite direction. Hopkins was perhaps induced to advance at a precocious rate in directions suggested by contemporary literary tendencies. The fortuitous confluence of Jesuit colloquy and Victorian dramatic monologue produced the distinctive *bidding* tone of his verse which is, therefore, not the result of his naïveté, but, more likely, of a hybrid and refined practice which happened to anticipate the direction which art has taken since his death.

[50] *Ibid.*, p. 160.

We have seen that Hopkins' " The Habit of Perfection " is an application of the senses in the form of a colloquy, or dramatic monologue. It is, moreover, composed of a series of paradoxes: the silence sings; shut lips are eloquent; eyes shelled with double dark find the light; the crust of the fast tastes best; and so on. The poem is composed of seven quatrains, each of which contains a paradox. Bridges, in the preface to the notes of the first edition of Hopkins' poems, observed, " It was an idiosyncrasy of [Hopkins'] mind to push everything to its logical extreme, and take pleasure in a paradoxical result." Hopkins' papers give abundant evidence that he delighted in paradox. Abbott mentions that Hopkins' entire family exhibited a " proneness to jocularity and juggling words," [51] which is manifest in Hopkins' delight in riddles, puns, and conundrums. A conundrum, of course, is really a paradox with the point of comparison withheld (e. g., What is black and white and red all over?—A newspaper.). It is another way to state a paradox (e. g., Strange that newspapers should be at once black and white and red!). Hopkins' native delight in paradox and word play is reinforced in his theological study. Are not all the central mysteries of Christianity paradoxes? And so Hopkins wrote those quaint and moving sermons—precise, convoluted, unsuccessful—revolving each tiny detail of Christ's life so as to view it from all possible angles and under all possible lights. Notes by Hopkins recording the effectiveness of his sermons are scattered throughout his papers. For example, there was a sermon delivered before his fellow priests on the text, " Then Jesus said, ' Make the men sit down.' " Hopkins ruefully notes, " This was a Dominical and was delivered on Mid-Lent Sunday March 11 1877 as far as the blue pencil mark. . . People laughed at it prodigiously, I saw some of them roll on their chairs with laughter. This made me lose the thread, so that I did not

[51] *Further Letters*, p. 130, *n2*.

deliver the last two paragraphs right but mixed things up. The last paragraph in which *Make the men sit down* is often repeated, far from having a good effect, made them roll more than ever." [52] It was Hopkins' delight in paradox which led to this disaster. He was considering the paradox of the power, as opposed to the mildness, of Christ's command when the audience dissolved in merriment. Hopkins was saying,

> The master had spoken: *Make the men sit down.* Our Lord had spoken but gently indeed: ποιήσατε τοὺς ἀνθρώπους ἀναπέσειν *Facite homines discumbere*, in your own language *Pawch i'r dynion eistedd i lawr*, which is little more than: *Make the people sit down*, but the evangelist more sternly tells the history: ἀναπέσον οὖν οἱ ἄνδρες *Discumbere ergo viri, Felly y gwyr a eistaddasant i lawr*, 5000 grown men like chidden children crouched to the ground at the word which made the men sit down. [53]

Hopkins' treatment seems inappropriate for his subject matter because the paradox which he treats with reverential wonder is not obvious. Christ said, " Make the men sit down," and they did so. The paradox of power and mildness in the words of Christ was too far fetched for Hopkins' audience.

Likewise, Hopkins preached a sermon on the story of St. Mary Magdalene with something less than success and, again, it was his delight in paradox which baffled his audience. The crux of this sermon concerns the forgiveness of Mary Magdalene's sins: Was she forgiven because she loved Christ, or did she love because she was forgiven? Hopkins' solution:

> She not only loved because she was forgiven, she was also forgiven because she loved: both things are true. When she came she came as a sinner, she had heard no forgiveness spoken, she came to get it, and to get it she shewed all that love: in this way then she was forgiven because she loved. On the other hand she knew of Christ's love, she knew he

[52] *Sermons and Devotional Writings*, p. 233.
[53] *Ibid.*, p. 231.

offered mercy to the sinner, to the great sinner great mercy, this love of his was first, mercy, forgiveness, *offered* forgiveness, on Christ's part came first and because he forgave her, that is offered to forgive her she loved: So then she loved because she was forgiven.[54]

The audience, understandably, had some difficulty in following Hopkins' explanation. He appended a note to this text: " After this sermon one of my penitents told me, with great simplicity, that I was not to be named in the same week with Fr. Clare. ' Well,' I said, ' and I will not be named in the same week. But did you hear it all? ' He said he did, only that he was sleeping for parts of it." [55] We see in Hopkins, then, a natural delight in paradox which found reinforcement and expression in theological study.

Hopkins is often accused of willful obscurity, but he himself explicitly demanded that a literary work must have a meaning which is completely clear. It is hard to justify his theory in the light of his practice unless we note that there is one kind of obscurity in a literary work which he will defend. If obscurity is used as a device to withhold the meaning from the reader until it bursts upon him, he will recommend it. He says, " One of two kinds of clearness one shd. have—either the meaning to be felt without effort as fast as one reads or else, if dark at first reading, when once made out *to explode*." [56] In an elementary sense, at least, Hopkins means that the meaning should explode in the way a riddle or the resolution of a paradox explodes. It is the surprise of the solution to a riddle which makes it delightful and Hopkins seems to claim that this effect of delightful surprise is a justification for obscurity in a literary work.

We have seen that Hopkins naturally used a conversational or dramatic situation in his verse which resulted in what he

[54] *Ibid.*, p. 83.
[55] *Ibid.*
[56] *Letters*, p. 90.

called the quality of *bidding* in his poems; that he delighted in
paradox; that he admired a meaning in poetry which *explodes*
like the meaning of a riddle. The form of poetry most congenial to these qualities is the epigram. Hopkins could turn
a neat epigram at an early age. Some examples written in
1864:

Modern Poets.
Our swans are now of such remorseless quill,
Themselves live singing and their hearers kill.

On a Poetess.
Miss M.'s a nightingale. 'Tis well
  Your simile I keep.
It is the way with Philomel
  To sing while others sleep.

(iv)
You ask why can't Clarissa hold her tongue.
Because she fears her fingers will be stung.

There is an epigrammatic effect in many of Hopkins' poems—
brevity, explosive meaning, a paradox or riddle implied in the
lines. Hopkins expresses a characteristic tendency of his
thought when he writes,

On one who borrowed his sermons.
Herclots' preachings I'll no longer hear:
They're out of date—lent sermons all the year.

This epigrammatic tendency is found in his mature poetry as
well. For example, a stanza from " The Silver Jubilee,"
written in 1876:

Not today we need lament
Your wealth of life is some way spent:
  Toil has shed round your head
Silver but for Jubilee.

From such concise word play it is only a step to the elliptical
paradoxes characteristic of " The Wreck of the Deutschland ":

Thou hast bound bones and veins in me, fastened in flesh,
And after it almost unmade, what with dread,
. . . .
Beyond saying sweet, past telling of tongue,
Thou art lightning and love, I found it, a winter and warm;
    Father and fondler of heart thou hast wrung:
. . . .
Flesh falls within sight of us, we, though our flower the
    same,
    Wave with the meadow, forget that there must
The sour scythe cringe, and the blear share come.

Here we have a welter of concise verbal and logical paradoxes:
God makes man in one sense, but undoes him in another; God
fondles the heart in one sense, but wrings it in another; the
flower which lives bears the shadow of death.

Hopkins, like Crashaw, received early and intensive training
in writing Latin and Greek epigrams. A friend of Hopkins
tells of their first meeting in grammar school: " That evening
we had elegiacs to do, for which Gerard had a very great
name, and much excitement was caused by ' the new fellow '
being also a dab at them, and the verses were done, and honours were claimed by our relative backers to be equally
divided between us." [57] Among the few examples of elegiac
verse by Hopkins that have been published is this one:

Tristi tu, memini, virgo cum sorte fuisti,
    Illo nec steterat tempore primus amor.
Jamque abeo: rursus tu sola relinqueris: ergo
    Tristior haec aetas; tristis et illa fuit.
Adsum gratus ego necopini apparitor ignis,
    Inter ego vacuas stella serena nives.

Hopkins also has a condensed version of this poem:

Tristis eras dum me venturum, Cythna, putares.
    Et veni et redeo: iam quoque tristis eris.
Adsum gratus ego necopini apparitor ignis,
    Inter ego gelidas stella serena nives.

[57] *Further Letters*, p. 394.

In both these poems (but more obviously in the shorter) we have typical epigrams. The poems are written in a conversational tone; both poems lead up to a concluding point of wit which takes the reader by surprise and hence the poems fall into two formal parts, exposition and conclusion; both poems aim for terseness.

Crashaw, too, devoted extensive study to the Latin epigram when he was a schoolboy. Austin Warren discovered through a collation of Crashaw's *Epigrammata Sacra* with the Sundays and Holy days of the Anglican Church Year that Crashaw's epigrammata are mainly the product of his three years at Pembroke College.[58] Composition in Latin verse therefore preceded composition in English for Crashaw. Wallerstein sees in these epigrams a fusion of the diction of Ovid and the technique of certain Renaissance rhetorical handbooks. She finds the epigrams to be one of the main influences on Crashaw's mature style. She says,

> Paradox is the dominant method [in the epigrams], giving color to all the other devices. The themes of Crashaw and the Jesuits deal wholly with the religious story, and it is perhaps for this reason, as well as by the mere process of stylization, that they use paradox so frequently; for to them life is a constant paradox between the forms of things and their allegorized meaning, the objects of this world being one extended allegory of the spiritual world; or between the values and ways of the life of this world as the man of the world reads and lives it, on the one side, and on the other, the values of the spirit.[59]

The use of the epigram which Wallerstein mentions as characteristic of the Jesuit writers of the Renaissance is somewhat different from the use of the epigram in Martial. For example, Martial's twelfth epigram from Book IV:

[58] Austin Warren, "Crashaw's Epigrammata Sacra," *JEGP*, **XXXIII** (1934), 236.
[59] Wallerstein, *Richard Crashaw*, p. 61.

Nulli, Thai, negas; sed si te non pudet istud,
  hoc saltem pudeat, thai, negare nihil.
(You deny no man, Thais. But if that does not put you to
shame, Thais, at least be ashamed to deny nothing.)

The form of this couplet is typical of Martial in that it is
conversational, concise, composed of an exposition and a conclusion, and wittily plays upon the word *nihil*. But it is also
typical in its worldly subject matter and biting attitude.
Crashaw copied the form of the epigram from Martial, but
not his subject matter and attitude. Prior to Crashaw, Martial's
style and subject matter had been widely used in England.[60]
The epigram which was adapted by the Jesuits in the seventeenth century, however, as Wallerstein mentions above, takes
its conversational situation, brevity, division into exposition
and conclusion, and witty word play from Martial—but not
its subject matter and attitude toward its subject matter. As
Scaliger says, " Epigrammatum autem genera tot sunt, quot
rerum." [61] Thus the Jesuits were able to use the technique
of Martial to treat theological ideas and Crashaw followed the
practice of the Jesuits.

When we compare Crashaw's Latin version of an epigram
to his English version of the same poem, keeping in mind that
the Latin version was probably written before the English,
it seems that Crashaw did not achieve epigrammatic brevity
so easily in English as in Latin. Compare the two epigrams
on " The Blessed Virgin's Bashfulness ":

In beatae Virginis verecundiam

In gremio, quaeris, cur sic sua lumina Virgo
  Ponat? ubi melius poneret illa, precor?
O ubi, quam coelo, melius sua lumina ponat?
  Despicit, *at coelum sic tamen illa videt.*

[60] See T. K. Whipple, *Martial and the English Epigram from Sir Thomas
Wyatt to Ben Jonson* (" University of California Publication in Modern
Philology "; Berkeley: University of California Press, 1925), Vol. X, No. 4.
[61] Scaliger, *Poetices Libri Septem* (London: apud Petrum Santandreanum,
1611), Bk. III, ch. 126.

> That on her lap she casts her humble Eye;
> 'Tis the sweet pride of her Humility.
> The faire star is well fixt, for where, o where,
> Could she have fixt it on a fairer spheare?
> 'Tis Heaven, 'tis Heaven she sees, Heavens God
>   there lyes
> She can see heaven, and ne're lift up her eyes:
> This new Guest to her Eyes new Lawes hath given,
> 'Twas once *looke up*, 'tis now *looke down* to
>   Heaven.

Scaliger says, despite the difficulty in defining the form of the epigram, that the two essential elements of the epigram are brevity and wit: "Epigrammatis virtutes peculiares: brevitas & argutia hanc Catullus non semper est assecutus: Martialis nusquam amisit." [62] It appears that Crashaw learned to be concise and witty in Latin and then tried to mold his English verse to that practice.

Hopkins, too, found it difficult in English to match the brevity and wit of the learned languages. His translation of these lines from the Greek anthology loses much of the compression of the Greek:

> Εἴ με φιλοῦντα φιλεῖς, δισσὴ χάρις εἰ δὲ μεμίσεις
> Τόσσον μὴ μισῇς, ὅσσον ἐγώ σε φιλῶ.

> (Love me as I love thee. O double sweet!
> But if thou hate me who love thee, albeit
>   Even thus I have the better of thee:
> Thou canst not hate so much as I do love thee.)

Clearly Hopkins is trying to copy the form of the Greek epigram—conversational situation, division into exposition and conclusion, wit—but his translation is not so concise as the original. Perhaps it was the precise, classical form of Dryden's epigram on Milton which led Hopkins to translate it into Latin:

⁶² *Ibid.*

> Three poets, in three distant ages born,
> Greece, Italy, and England did adorn.
> The first in loftiness of thought surpass'd
> The next in majesty, in both the last.
> The force of Nature could no farther go;
> To make a third she joined the former two.

> (Aevo diversi tres et regione poetae
>   Hellados, Ausoniae sunt Britonumque decus.
> Ardor in hoc animi, majestas praestat in illo,
>   Tertius ingenio iunxit untrumque suo.
> Scilicet inventrix cedens Natura labori
>   "Quidquid erant isti" dixerat "unus eris.")

Hopkins is able to sharpen the wit, to make the meaning more explosive, in Latin, but he does not improve the brevity of Dryden.

Years of practice at composition in Latin in the style of Martial had a great effect on Crashaw's English style, and it can hardly have left Hopkins' style uninfluenced—especially when, as Wallerstein points out, the form of the epigram is especially congenial to Jesuit ideas. The points of similarity, therefore, between the poetic styles of Crashaw and of Hopkins include: (1) the tendency to treat theological ideas in sensual terms, (2) a characteristic mode of speech resembling a religious colloquy which leads to what Hopkins calls the quality of *bidding*, (3) a delight in paradox which leads to what Hopkins calls explosive meaning, or perhaps obscurity, (4) epigrammatic compression and witty word play. These characteristics may be attributed, at least in part, to the common influence of Loyola and Martial on both writers. From Loyola both men learned that the apprehension of a theological idea through the senses by means of the composition of place and the application of the senses leads to a more forcible assent to the theological idea. From Loyola, too, they learned the practice of the religious colloquy which, if translated into verse, leads to a colloquial or conversational style. From

Martial they learned the form of the epigram, its brevity and wit. Crashaw acquired these attitudes and skills when critical taste was tending away from sympathy with such a poetic style and his reputation suffered an eclipse until Grierson and Eliot restored it in the 1920's. Hopkins, on the other hand, encountered these same ideas when they were congruent to the literary trends of his time. In the religious colloquy of Loyola, he found reinforcement of the ideas which supported the use of dramatic monologue, the distinctive voice of the poetry of experience. In the application of the senses, he found reinforcement of the psychology of Newman, fore-shadowing the taste for a direct sensuous apprehension of thought. In Martial's paradox and word play, he found a practice congenial to his own temperament, well designed for the expression of theological ideas which occupied him, and—incidentally—foresaw thereby the kind of poetry dear to the psychological critics of the twentieth century because it seems to express a state of tension and psychical poise. Far from being divorced from all tradition, the peculiar style of Hop-kins is largely the result of a fortuitous confluence of tradi-tions which led him to push forward at a precocious rate in directions already defined in Victorian art.

Index

GERARD MANLEY HOPKINS: The Classical Background and Critical Reception of His Work
By Todd K. Bender

designer:	Edward King
typesetter:	J. H. Furst Company
typefaces:	Janson, Goudy
printer:	J. H. Furst Company
paper:	Olde Style Wove
binder:	Moore & Co.
cover material:	Arrestox B 41000